How to train a puppy

This book includes:

The beginners' guide to the art of perfect dog training

+

Professional approach to handling and training your dog

By Jennifer Dogget

Table of Contents

The beginners' guide to the art of perfect dog training

Professional approach to handling and training your dog

How to train a puppy

The beginners guide to the art of realizing perfect dog training. Learn the basics of commands and tricks with tips on how to exercise the perfect dog.

By Jennifer Dogget

INTRODUCTION

Congratulations -- It is time to bring home your new pup! You are aware of how significant socialization and great behaviour is to get a household pet, and you are spent in establishing a new puppy obedience training regime on your house right from the beginning. Additionally, puppy training builds a bond between a dog and his new human family. However, where do you begin?

Like parenting, even in house dog training can be difficult and challenging. Most of us love the ideal dog that's careful, nevertheless able to stay calm and independent. And like people, dogs arrive with their very own different characters, strengths and flaws.

Creating a connection with your fur creature comes simple but in house dog training? That is tough. To be able to achieve dog obedience at the house it is crucial that you initially make an environment that's conducive to understanding. The remainder is all about inviting your friend to produce skills which are beneficial to your life.

Being a fantastic pet is a little like becoming a life coach, it takes several'atta boys' and tender demeanour, instead of being the large, scary boss which scares you into submission. Knowing dog behaviour can be vitally important to be able to train them . Beneath, you will find out what there is to understand in attaining dog in the house and how to make it stand out.

9

CHAPTER ONE:
BEFORE GETTING A PUPPY

THINK IT THROUGH BEFORE GETTING A DOG

People get puppies for many different motives: companionship, guarding functions, searching, support functions and all around the world, people are getting to be pet owners for the very first time in their own lives. Humane shelters and adoption agencies are filled with abandoned puppies, and until you're tempted to have a dog house, there are numerous things which you ought to think on.

Few Things can tug at our hearts just as far as the eyes of an abandoned dog or pup, as well as the notion of all of the unconditional love puppy companions, must provide can frequently cause us to create spontaneous decisions without even permitting us to think sensibly. A lot of men and women who choose dogs dwelling without thinking it through ideally might find themselves not able to take care of the puppy and abandoning it.

Dedication and alongside the unconditional love and tranquility come to a wide variety of duties. As a pet owner, you're ultimately accountable for supplying all of your pet needs like water, food, care and health care if he wants it. The most home trained of puppies may have the occasional injury in your home, and you might need to be ready to clean up after your puppy when he is sick or whenever you take him out for a stroll.

Work to seek out your favorite shoes are chewed to a pulp or maybe to come across the rug in shreds. If your pet is still an obsessive barker, you ought to be ready to devote a whole lot of time handling the matter, or you'll have a lot of unhappy neighbors in your situation.

Before you draw those Adoption, documents take a good look at what it means to have a puppy. Below are some factors you should consider when making that final choice:

Should I get a Dog?

If You're an athletic and Lively individual or you've got such an individual in your family, then, you can look at getting a puppy. If a household contains busy men and women that are always glued to the tv or computer afterwards, a puppy might not be such a fantastic idea. Dogs require regular daily walks, for no less than half an hour. You'll also need to pick up after your puppy in your steps. Kids and teens eager to receive a puppy will amaze you with guarantees about how they will do whatever required to care for the dog ought to be taken with a pinch of salt. What generally will occur following the novelty of having a puppy wanes off is you will be left with the job of caring for your dog.

Dogs Aren't cheap to maintain You'll need to have the ability to feed your pet a fantastic excellent diet, and there are several different costs associated with having a puppy: tick and flea remedies, kennel coasts in case you go on holiday, accessories and toys along with veterinary care if your pet gets ill. If your pet never gets sick in his/her life that you will still accept him for veterinary vaccinations and checkups and all these items aren't affordable.

If you are a Busy individual with hardly any free time, you shouldn't find a puppy. Dogs are social creatures that require companionship and time; they do not do well if left alone for extended intervals. Dogs left to their own devices do and can create behavioural problems like destructive chewing gum and aggression.

Should I get a dog for the children?

If you have a toddler or infant in the home, you must postpone obtaining a puppy. Young children and infants are a part of a couple without incorporating a puppy to the mixture. Not all dogs are great with kids rather than all kids know how to act around dogs.

If Your child understands the meaning of obligation and is about 12 years old, so this might be a fantastic environment to get a puppy into. Dogs are excellent for kids in the ideal conditions, and they're able to teach kids a lot of items in addition to supplying them. Adolescents, in particular, can benefit from owning and caring for a puppy since they are in an age when demonstrating affection to their parents could be regarded as "uncool" within their age category. Therefore, a dog could offer an emotional outlet for your kid. Teens are often going through a tumultuous time in their growth so that they might not be consistent with caring for a puppy. If you wish to receive a dog to your kids, be sure you're ready to have the duty of caring for this if or if your kids eliminate interest. Children could be unpredictable, so be sure that you're prepared for it.

As Soon as You've determined you can provide a puppy with a fantastic home for your remainder of its life, it is time to see local adoption facilities to pick your dog. Try and do some research as much as possible concerning the area and the puppies out there. Speak to staff along with other puppy owners and explore some dog breeds you are interested in to detect some other characters traits or disorders they're predisposed to. In regard to doing your homework before bringing a puppy into your house, there's not any dumb question. Do not reluctant to ask anything that you like on dog ownership.

Even In the event, you decide you enjoy a specific breed's traits, and then you ought to keep in mind that puppies are people and only because a puppy is a member of a particular breed famous for a specific trait, does not necessarily imply The puppy will take this attribute. The internet is filled with valuable information concerning the many facets of dog owners take advantage of it and see as far as possible.

TEACH YOURSELF ON HOW TO TRAIN YOUR NEW PUPPY

A puppy is a beautiful addition to your house, but many new owners don't see the significance of training a puppy along with an unchecked puppy could develop to a tumultuous and temperamental mature dog. Dog obedience training must start the moment the puppy arrives in the house and keep gently to ensure proper behaviour is strengthened and poor behaviour is always forbidden. Before bringing the pup home, the household needs to pre-determine the principles and be sure these principles have been adhered to by everybody. There are no days away if training puppies and decent training will enhance the puppy's bond and connection with the whole family. The puppy will learn how to trust and follow their proprietor at each control, and this contributes to a nicely behaved, controllable puppy.

Obedience training ensures the dog understands to obey its grasp and may have significant impacts on the protection of a pet. A well-trained dog won't ever run into visitors while on a stroll using its proprietor because all its master needs to perform with command respect and obedience will be to complete a word, word or provide a gesture. A real dog is apt to become uncontrollable and poses a threat to itself and others. A real dog could be erratic and incline to jump at people and conduct across streets and even attempt to attack individuals or creatures it doesn't understand. Training a puppy is essential in several ways as appropriate instruction can cut the odds of a household becoming overwhelmed with all the maintenance of a disobedient puppy and neglecting or left it. Obedient dogs are more prone to spend some time with and maybe trusted with all the very young, older or infirm. They are not as inclined to ruin furniture, bark or display hostility.

Dog training Ought to Be positive and Rewarding for both dog and owner. If a puppy completes a job successfully, he must get a reward which will promote him to replicate this learned behaviour. Treats and tidbits are frequently the quickest way to lure a dog to carry out a control and puppy training could be useful if started in the home, but a lot of individuals don't have sufficient time to devote these hardcore coaching. Often, specialist obedience training courses are a much better idea unless the proprietor has some expertise or assist in educating their puppy.

Regular obedience training Generally starts with simple commands like "sit" and "remain", but more Complicated controls are usually educated at a subsequent stage. Training a puppy may have many paths like teaching him to act well in societal Events, on a walk or at the house. The puppy Ought to Be introduced to Lots of people and other puppies as you can, and this can be accomplished in Busy parks or even obedience classes. An Operator Shouldn't train their puppy To obey anger or anxiety but instead motivate them to learn self-control For more positive factors. Training a puppy could prevent injuries and save its own life, so it must be accomplished when possible.

WHEN TO GET A DOG

You may need a puppy, but think - would a puppy wish to be with you at this moment in your lifetime? Needing a puppy and getting one are two entirely different matters. Whether you select an adult dog or a pet, you need to take into consideration your situation at the appropriate moment. There are some facts to take into account before welcoming a puppy in your house - with the opportunity to understand how to train your dog or puppy is among the most essential.

Get the time right

Are you prepared to receive a puppy? The time Might Not Be perfect for one if you're:

- Moving home or expected to go on vacation.
- Occupied at work and well.
- Changing occupations or facing job loss.
- From the throes of an illness.
- Separating from the spouse or distress bereavement.
- Anticipating a baby.
- Coming of a significant family party that can disturb your patterns and boost household action or sound levels.

There are always exceptions, and several men and women find relaxation in their pets occasionally when they're suffering anxiety. Such owners might feel, though they are in chaos, their pets aren't suffering because they stay fed and cared for. But pets don't believe that their owners' worries and may stress. All these anxieties can manifest in behaviour like attention-seeking or soil around the house.

You must be in a place both emotionally and professionally to supply a safe and harmonious house to some other dog.

Vacations

Wait until you've been off before obtaining a puppy since he will endure upheaval double in a brief space of time initially once you eliminate him away from his former house, and then once you vanish and leave him at a boarding kennel or using a carer. To stay mentally and emotionally well, a new pet demands a fantastic deal of time to sit and feel safe in his new residence.

Dog availability

It's sometimes not as easy to get a puppy as you may envision for Many reasons:

- If you would like a Specific breed, colour or gender of a puppy, it may not be accessible, and you might need to register a particular requirement using a Breeder so that if a creature is available, you've got the first option.
- Puppy accessibility consistently is determined by breeding seasons.
- There might not instantly be the specific kind of puppy you need at rescue facilities.
- Puppies are inclined to be in significant demand at rescue facilities, and you might need to wait.

Make sure it's the ideal time to receive a puppy for all of the family.

KNOW ABOUT BREED CHARACTERISTICS BEFORE GETTING A DOG

Adding a puppy for your loved ones is a significant decision and one which warrants study and careful consideration. A lot of adults wish to believe that magic moment when they consider these soft dog eyes for the very first time and also feel an immediate connection. There's not anything wrong with this feeling per state. What dog fan does not wish to locate a fantastic companion that's an ideal fit?

On the other hand, the sad reality is what generally occurs when you receive a puppy on feelings, is that instant is simply a minute. When you choose your new pal Rory house, the daily pattern takes its toll, and suddenly you've got a dog in your hands that isn't a fantastic match for your existing way of life. There is nothing unfeeling about performing some research before going to adopt a puppy. In reality, understanding precisely what you're searching for and exactly what it is possible to handle makes the minute of relationship that much sweeter since you genuinely do understand you have discovered a fantastic companion to talk about your life. You owe it to yourself and your puppy to have a great idea about what you are getting into until you choose Rory house.

Some Main things to consider are the qualities of your prospective pet's breed, even when you're considering obtaining a mixed strain. Also, though the best features of each breed tend to come to the fore at mutts, these puppies may still display dominant breed characteristics so that it's always worth some time to know about what you're receiving. Breed features have an enormous influence on the puppy's character, and you and your lifetime. Are you currently able to work out a top drive strain? Are you presently ready to deal with a working breed that enjoys nothing more than see and bark at all and enter your stuff? Are you going to be about with sufficient frequency to provide a needy dog with the right quantity of attention?

An Apartment Way I Desire a Little Dog, Right?

Some individuals will take their present living situation into account when adopting a puppy. They believe that a little dog is fantastic for an apartment or condominium, while a giant dog is much better positioned in a house with a lawn. While deciding on puppy suitability according to dimensions does workout at a lot of instances, there are a few tiny breeds which genuinely do not perform as well in flats. That is, again, because of strain attributes. By way of instance, a Jack Russell terrier is a little puppy so he ought to work good in a flat. That the Jack Russell's breed attributes aren't that ideal for flat or even town dwelling. These puppies possess a strong hunting drive, plus they call for a great deal of focus from you outside activity, exercise and area to be great companions. They may be aggressive toward other dogs, which may result in a lot of problems in a snug environment like a town.

On the other hand, little dogs ideal for apartment living are inclined to be associates of their toy' pet group. Many dogs in this class are composed and flirty, and they do not call for a fantastic deal of exercise, sometimes, excessive focus. If you live alone in a flat or are getting on in years, a Chihuahua may be a tremendous selection. While Chihuahuas have adverse traits (as does some other strain) which comprise being leery of different dogs and humans, they're incredibly faithful to their owners and probably won't result in harm should they jump on you to say hello.

When You've Got Your Your Lifestyle Permits, A Larger Breed Might Be You

The working set of dog breeds, including Dobermans, both Australian and German Shepherds, Huskies and Rottweilers, call for a whole lot of exercise and comprehension of the character. Active working fashions exhibited within this class include focusing on placing a hole on your sofa or chewing via a lamp chord as you're on the job. Working dogs which have strong herding characteristics like Border Collies are usually not suited to city dwelling, while within a flat or a home. These kinds of dogs typically call for a great deal of room to work out inside, and you might find Rory attempting to ditch the yard furniture.

Each dog Breeds mentioned and also the number of different strains available has numerous Fantastic features which make them hot and loving companies, Especially with excellent training. Additionally, It's not a complete certainty That any specific puppy won't be a fantastic companion for you personally if Rory's Principal breed attributes do not generally mesh with the way you live Or living circumstances. But because oblivious dog/human Relationships occur with too much frequency, so being alert to the Exercise and care requirements of pet breeds as well as what their strain Attributes may mean for you and your lifetime, will help you create A solid decision that contributes to this 15,000-year-old mysterious connection Between man and dog.

THINGS TO THINK ABOUT BEFORE GETTING A DOG

Thinking of a dog or puppy addition to the household. Hoping to get a furry bundle of joy? That is great, but do you think this through carefully? It is a significant responsibility; here are a couple of things to consider before taking the plunge.

1. What type of dog do you desire?

Be sure to think about what kind of dog you desire. Each strain is different about how clever they are, how large they make, how favourable they tend to be, just how much exercise they want, etc.. If you're interested in finding a specific breed, look at a rescue but should you would like to buy from a breeder, check their references and be sure that they do whatever they're predicted to, then this varies with strain. No matter what you do, ensure that you research the breed you're thinking about, even a mix in case you are aware of what the mixture is.

2. Do you have the money?

Possessing a puppy can at minimum be an effect on your financial plan and at worst a real cost occasionally. Only a trip for vaccinations could quickly run within a hundred bucks. Then, of course, there's food and other equipment. According to my experience and survey of pet products, I guess your start-up costs for food and supplies will be approximately 200 bucks. I've got a 25 pound Sheltie. His meals function out to be around 15 dollars each month. Veterinarian bills operate about 200 dollars each year; this includes an ill trip or 2; additionally, heartworm and flea and tick protection conduct approximately 10 dollars each month. He has dressed twice per year for around 80 bucks; we can do this but opt not to. We invest on average about 50 dollars each month, barring any substantial illness or harm.

3. Would you enjoy poop?

Puppies poop each time they consume so that you're looking at three or four times every day. An adult dog, will likely "move" two - 3 times every day. The meals that a puppy eats includes a bearing on how much faeces he can create — the more affordable the meals, the longer the stool. Therefore, in the event you purchase cheap meals, you may cover it at the ending. This substance can accumulate quickly so that you genuinely will need to wash up at least one time every day. Take my advice. Clean up after every moment, it will make life much more straightforward and keeps the lawn clean also.

4. Would you want to work out?

Any dog loves a stroll and ought to have one. Some breeds require this, and without that, your dog might have behaviour issues, like chewing or excessive barking. You need to plan on a regular walking program, mainly if your breed requires a particular amount of exercise, which breed research will show.

5. Would you want to sleep late?

Dogs often are morning folks. That is not to mention a dog regularly must get up, but most do cause they have to go potty. Another factor to consider is that a puppy might not sleep during the evening and you might need to wake up and take the small critter out for a potty break; this isn't the most enjoyable on a chilly night. Keep in mind this, if you genuinely prefer to sleep a puppy may not be the ideal alternative.

6. Would you enjoy or need to travel?

You can not leave your pet once you travel you will either need to have a pet sitter come to the home or take him into a buddy or even a kennel. A kennel will cost you approximately 25 to 50 dollars each day based on the kind of kennel as well as also the size of their dog. You will find resorts that allow dogs, even if you'll have the time while your off to tend for her.

7. Do you intend on other household improvements soon?

If you've got an infant in the home or even a toddler, including a puppy to the combination might not be the best thought. For starters, the puppy will be another requirement for your focus, in addition to the brand new pet may become envious of their new siblings.

8. When do you intend on getting this particular dog?

It's not a fantastic idea to bring a new puppy or dog to the home around an Important holiday, such as Christmas. There's too much happening, also Many distractions. The same goes for birthdays. If You Would like to get a Brand new dog around a substantial occasion, like these, take action After and create a particular event from it, which it'll be!

CHAPTER TWO:
MEET YOUR PUPPY

MEETING YOUR DOG FOR THE FIRST TIME

Hooray! You discovered a puppy you want to take home. Here are a few things for fulfilling a puppy for the very first time.

Allow your dog approach you

After meeting a puppy, it is essential to be calm and move slow. Your initial Instinct is to operate towards the puppy together with open arms, but maybe not too quickly! Approaching a puppy, this manner may startle them, and it may come off too intimidating. Instead, maintain a pure position, and make it possible for the dog to return to you. You ought to avoid coming across too fearful, however, because this may lead your dog to become defensive. Be mindful, yet convinced, when fulfilling a puppy for the very first time.

Let your dog sniff you

Allowing yourself to some brand new dog is about knowing the Dog's instincts. Dogs have a very keen sense of smell. They use odour to comprehend and make decisions regarding their surroundings. In only a couple of weeks, a puppy can find an understanding of the sex, health, as well as the background of some other dog. When a puppy sniffs an individual, they could ascertain whether that individual has a pet of their own, in which at the area the individual might reside, and much more. They're also able to select upon an individual's unique odour to run their memory regarding if and if they have met before! To allow a dog sniff you, then do not stretch your hands to your face. Instead, let the dog approach you and scatter your hands in their terms.

Don't Pet his head

When meeting a puppy, always take care to admire their boundaries. Petting on the head could be threatening to get a puppy, particularly when the individual petting them is an entire stranger. As opposed to reaching for his mind straight away, begin with patting them lightly on their shoulders or back. Following that, it is possible to work your way in their face if they're familiar with it.

Pay attention to body language

The same as people, dogs communicate through human language. In regards to decoding dog anatomy, we've got a couple of hints. Generally, things such as a curved figure, wagging tail, and even excitedly circling about you is a fantastic indication; it means that they wish to get to understand you. Bowing down front legs stretched is a gesture which says "Play !". Look out for anything which may suggest a threatening or aggressive disposition, like revealing a rigid, vertical tail.

Additionally, it is essential to know that all dogs respond differently to pressure. Some could express distress or nervousness from licking their lips or even yawning. This is deemed normal behaviour for a puppy who's put at an unfamiliar or stressful circumstance.

Use a calm, low voice when meeting a puppy

It is typical for people to use "baby talk" when initially meeting a puppy. Nevertheless, the appropriate way to approach a puppy would be to talk in your regular voice. Keep it low and calm. Employing a high pitched voice could indicate weakness In addition to stress out your dog. Establish your connection right from The beginning by exuding confidence and esteem for any new pet you match.

BRINGING YOUR PUPPY HOME - THE FIRST NIGHT

You thought you wanted a pup, but nowadays he's complaining and yelling, and you can not get any sleep. Before you choose to eliminate the small critter, understand precisely what's happening with your furry friend.

Dogs Are pack animals, and you've just split the young puppy from his loved ones. If you're likely to be a suitable puppy coach, you must know he is only acting normal. He knows by intuition that being separated from his loved ones is reckless and is searching for his bunch.

The very best way to manage your pet's first nighttime is with preparation. After he's fun with his new residence, fulfilling his new household, be sure that you take his water and food of at least four weeks before your bedtime. Do not let him nap in this period because if you do, then he is going to be prepared to play if you would like to go to sleep soundly.

The very best approach to train your pup, be sure he spends the night in the area. He wants to be constantly aware that you're his brand new pack leader. In case the breeder had begun cage training, then place the crate into your area for the evening. Otherwise, direct him something and put an old blanket or blouse with your odour. It's not a fantastic thought to let them sleep on the mattress since he'll take care of this behaviour as usual.

Puppies do not generally soil the place where they sleep, but It's an excellent thought to have up a couple of times in the night to help alleviate his little bladder. Furthermore, if he can complain in the nighttime, it's excellent to understand the distinction between a shout for attention along with a cry for a toilet break. When it's been a few hours because he left a noise, this is a fantastic indication that the puppy should visit the toilet. If he yells in other times, reach down and give him a swift reassurance. Do not pick up to cuddle him because this isn't appropriate reinforcement and may create problems in the future. If it persists, the very best thing would be to dismiss him. I know this sounds mean. However, you do not wish to fortify a stern, subsequently sympathetic regular that amuses the pet. He'll eventually find out that crying at night does not have any benefits.

Most In the early hours, get up quickly and pick up the pup and take the puppy out to do his enterprise. Should you allow him to walk his, He might another more suitable place on the way.

INTRODUCE YOUR PUPPY TO THE WORLD

Socializing your pet is a significant step in helping him find his place in the realm of people and other puppies.

A puppy naturally starts socializing within the mess. But when he is taken out of the clutter, the socialization process must continue in his new surroundings.

You want your pet to develop confident and be comfortable in his environment. Willing to meet strangers with no cowering. Playful and lively using fresh dogs. Never competitive when encountering an unknown situation.

=== Adding Your Puppy To New People ===

Your Puppy will develop in a world filled with individuals. This is a natural element of the world. When it's the children next door glancing above the fence. Or the UPS deliveryman position at the front door. Or friends who've come to see.

You want your pet to delight in such experiences and take all of them in stride.

By Exposing him as many distinct individuals as you can while he is still between 6 and 12 months old, it's possible to assist him to socialize.

Invite Friends or acquaintances over to fulfil your pet. Have them down to his flat and provide him with a favorite dog biscuit. Be sure they don't utilize any sudden movements which may frighten him. And ensure your puppy receives compliments for taking the bite. This can help discourage bitterness and anxiety.

Take him for walks into the playground or the Pet shop or on the area, where he could meet new men and women. If strangers request to pet him, make sure you praise your pet for his excellent behaviour and for staying calm.

Require him to obedience classes, where he will be around other people and dogs. If your pet seems to fear in the middle of all of the action, do not force the problem. You could always try again later. But be sure that you don't guarantee him whether he is fearful, possibly. This is only going to reinforce the behaviour.

Fundamentally, You would like to make the most of every chance to expose your pet to new individuals. Every new adventure will give rise to his developing confidence.

=== Adding Your Puppy To New Dogs ===

A Puppy learns to interact with his or her siblings. This interaction helps him understand to inhibit his scratching and also create self-control. Additionally, it helps your pet to expend all of the puppy energy, which makes him less hyperactive and destructive to your home.

What do you do to assist him after he has left the mess?

Puppy Kindergarten and pup training are equally excellent techniques to maintain him interacting with dogs. A neighborhood puppy training class is also a fantastic option. Or maybe you try going down to your closest dog park, that is almost always an excellent place to work out your pup while he satisfies other dogs.

All these excursions Ought to Be fun, with no Pressure in your pet to carry out. Allow him to socialize with all the other dogs in his refuge.

If none of the work for you, see If you're able to Locate a doggy day maintenance service in your region. It's possible to shed off your puppy in your way to operate and let him spend the afternoon interacting and playing with other dogs before you pick up him in your way house. After a week is good, more frequently in the event, you'd enjoy.

In the end, if you presently have an older dog at home, often he will provide all of the drama and advice your pet requirements.

=== Adding Your Puppy To New Situations ===

The Contemporary world is filled with stimulation for a pup. You will find auto excursions, televisions, vacuum cleaner, doorbells, screaming infants, fireworks, trips to the veterinarian, music and countless other brand new adventures.

Expose your pup to as a number of these scenarios as you can. The longer, the better.

Don't push him to those adventures. Allow him to deal with them in his or her leisure. When he responds with dread, do not give him the wrong message from reassuring him. This reinforces his anxiety and will help it become even more challenging for him to cope with additional new scenarios.

Socializing Your pet should be an enjoyable procedure. Keep after it, and You'll have a serene, positive, and friendly household companion.

CHAPTER THREE:
DOG PSYCHOLOGY AND BEHAVIOUR

UNDERSTANDING DOG PSYCHOLOGY

Most people will have undergone some dog psychology. Dogs have a means of getting us people to do precisely what they desire. The unintelligent puppy you understand is going to have the ability to beg off the food you with that look in their eyes which you can not resist.

Having lived together across generations puppies have learned to speak with people and let's know what they desire. In case your dog thinks it is time for a stroll at the park, then he will bring his leash, even if he wishes to play fetch, then he will bring you his ball. All activities we all take for granted nevertheless reveal the puppy is capable of learning complicated behaviour.

Even though Dogs may comprehend a surprising number of body and verbal language, pet psychology and also how they process information is slightly different from us people.

They have more exceptional ability to view in reduced light and can pinpoint both smells and sounds correctly, and they interpret cause and effect in a very different manner.

Associating A stimulus with an answer is quite a bit more persistent in puppies, but people can alter an undesirable reaction.

Suppose you select His leash up; he will think he is going for a stroll. Select his ball up, and he will likely know he is going for a stroll and playing catch. But if you then pick up his food bowl he will be wholly confused and not know exactly what to do, mind you would I.

Should you follow a specific Pattern of events frequently, your puppy will learn what is coming, but he can not know whether that series of events is busted. People can adapt to those changes, and puppies do not process the data in precisely the same manner.

Dogs can find commands by adhering to the design of the Voice and translating hand gestures which accompany these controls. Sit, stay, come, lie down, and are clear examples but puppies may also be educated more complex behaviour as rescue dogs for the blind and support dogs reveal.

Though It's possible to educate dogs all Sorts of things, occasionally what appears evident to people, like not eating a decaying bunny, you might not ever have the ability to instruct your pet. They can not relate the reason for the rabbit, to function as the consequence of this upset stomach that occurs at a subsequent moment.

Just recall dog psychology and How that they believe different from the way we know life and even We attempt to view our dog occasionally as an individual, to these, we're just another dog.

PUPPYHOOD AND BEHAVIOURAL DEVELOPMENT

Puppyhood can be divided into four main phases:

- Neonatal

- Transitional

- Socialization

- Juvenile

Neonatal

This interval starts at the beginning and the last 14 days. In this period, the puppy is defenceless but adapted to his surroundings. He's been fitted from arrival with several traits which let him do what he wants to endure: nourish and receive his mother's attention.

His nervous system remains predominantly Underdeveloped, and even while his sense of smell, taste and touch exist, he's deaf and blind. One important mechanism is that the distress call: it is a different, instinctual call that the puppy makes when he encounters discomfort, like becoming lost. Dogs are born with this call, and also the urge develops a max of five months following arrival. The mum's instinctual result of the phone begins at the arrival of the final puppy of her mess and ends two weeks after, in the conclusion of the neonatal phase of her clutter's lifestyle. She'll reply to her dogs' requirements, and just during the particular period of pregnancy. If a puppy gets dropped before the previous person is born, his shouts will probably be dismissed; only a 17-day old pup makes precisely the same call.

The puppy can clumsily roll around, generally at a circular direction, to never stray away from his mommy. Since dogs at this age continue to be deaf and blind, their neural network does not allow for much instruction. This said it'd been proven that pups (even wolf pups) managed by people in this time are far more inclined to take care of anxiety in adulthood, more difficult to people and all-around much better learners compared to pups who've been treated very little or just after the specified period.

Transitional

This period starts before the conclusion of the short period and finishes in less or more 30 days of existence (two months in length).

This period, the puppy's eyes (between 10-16) and ears (between 18-20) open. This marks the transition from a wholly dependent newborn to a different puppy. Adult behaviours (tail wagging, growling, different play behaviours, pouncing.) begin to form now along with also the mom stops reacting to the distress call of her pups. The startle reaction to loud sounds is current, and although vision is terrible, the puppy can follow moving objects. The dogs begin to walk and at the wild, and this is the era where the today ambulatory dogs emerge in the den to the very first time.

Socialization

This period also referred to as the imprinting period, goes in the third week of existence most of the way into the 12th. It's essential to be aware that in wolves, this age lasts just under three months, that is about 30 percent of the time that it dogs. This simple fact permits individuals to desensitize shepherds to creatures they would typically feel likely to search and consume (horses, horses.) and instead instill in them the tendency to safeguard and protect those creatures.

The provisions socialization and imprinting are very quiet Hot words inside the training area, and with good reason! This vital period in a creature's life defines the person they will develop to become.

Learning skill and socialization are in Their peak in that time, the puppy learns precisely what species he belongs to according to the societal interactions lived in this age. He begins to move less, profits more ability along with a willingness to research everywhere and everything.

During that time, the puppy Becomes connected not just to people, for example, his littermates and handler(s), but also into areas, his surroundings and inanimate objects.

Given a puppy's inherent fascination at this era, and raised learning capability, handlers and coaches will need to be somewhat cautious in regards to traumatic events due anxiety towards something dissipates in that era is hard to change, as is all, bad or good, that's learned at that moment.

This era is the best time to Begin Housetraining a puppy, even since they are attracted to the odour of faeces and urine, and so begin preferring to remove where these odours can be located.

So far as behaviour is concerned, this is the most significant period from the dog's development. Many ethologists and behaviorists concur that though the imprinting phase is quite long at the puppy, the pup is the most accessible between the fifth and third week of existence. In this period, the dogs won't oppose to being treated. Following the fifth week, they begin to become more stressed. After the 12th week, managing an inadequately socialized puppy gets quite hard.

Juvenile

This interval extends from the end of this socialization phase up till puberty (between 6-12 weeks old). Ethologically talking, dogs could be considered lasting teens. They keep juvenile behaviours (like the capability to bark) into maturity and become sexually healthy without becoming fully emotionally mature.

While It's true that the Imprinting period is finished, pups this era continue to be sensitive to new items, whether or maybe not, so care has to be taken to prevent social regression which could cause anxiety and timidity. Harsh treatment (for example sharp "adjustments" in obedience training) could be particularly harmful, resulting in, in most probability, irreparable harm.

Studies appear to attest to the existence of a fifth interval, the period, which can be affected by the surroundings that the gestating female is at and the way she responds to it. It's well documented that stress adversely impacts both mother and her unborn pups, however also the specific effects in puppies have yet to be widely researched.

For a successful Socialization process, that the handler must expose the pup to as many secure scenarios and surroundings as possible. Equipped with high-value positive reinforcement (toys, treats.), the controller needs to present the puppy to a lot of dogs and people, rewarding a fantastic response and strategy.

The puppies that the pup meets must be well socialized rather than responsive or competitive.

One must maintain size and power level in your mind if you're searching for appropriate playmates for your young puppy; a seven days old Miniature Pinscher and a five-month-old Rottweiler might not be the ideal match!

Vaccinations also need to be considered. Ahead of the comprehensive vaccination series was administered, it's ideal for maintaining the pup from high-risk places like dog parks and pet classes. The puppies deemed suitable for interacting with a puppy has to be healthful.

Vaccine schedules change considerably, but usually, the protocol begins at eight months and can be completed in about 16 weeks. A deficiency of exposure to the external world and all its myriad stimulation has a damaging influence in an imprinting pup and is going to lead to a puppy who's pulled, lacks adequate societal behaviour and interrupts anything fresh.

This brings us into some very highly contested debate: if is a pup prepared to be adopted out into the family?

Some Experts assert that sooner (around six months old) at the imprinting interval is higher, it permits the puppy to nevertheless be emotionally malleable as it moves to its new surroundings. Other people assert that carrying away a pup away from its littermates earlier 7-8 months old makes them socially insufficient since it robs them with different dogs. Various studies have revealed that dogs who are weaned with their mom rather than rehomed until approximately 12 months old have better societal etiquette (like higher sting inhibition) than people put in new homes sooner.

At whatever age you choose to receive your puppy, bear in mind that socialization is a lifelong affair; and although it's true which "erasing" a faulty upbringing is quite hard, with all the right tools it is not impossible.

Make it enjoyable, keep it positive, and you're going to have a well-adjusted and happy pet!

PAEDOMORPHISM AND BEHAVIOURAL DEVELOPMENT

Paedomorphism is that the retention of juvenile characteristics or traits to adulthood, usually brought on by neoteny, the postponed growth of a creature. The animal undergoes puberty to achieve sexual maturity, however, keeps particular juvenile bodily or emotional traits.

If the genes which determine adulthood, present mutations, the animal will grow to, say, one year old, and that is going to be regarded as normal adult growth for this line. The development of all of the pet breeds we see now is due to mutations to selection for all these genes.

Mutation and selection do not demand only one attribute, but a lot of others too, desired or not. The most obvious example of this is sometimes observed at Belyaev's foxes. From the '50s," Dr Belyaev, a Russian physiologist and geneticist, put out to see how much time it would require him to domesticate a species' from scratch fully'. Considering that the gorgeous dark charcoal coat of the silver fox (a melanistic variant of the well-known red fox) was prized in Russia," Dr Belyaev and his group had effortless access to substantial numbers of those animals. However, humility towards people was not the only attribute that distinguished those foxes in their undomesticated counterparts. After a few years, the foxes began to exhibit dog-like bodily features like a curly (spitz) tail, tan, floppy ears, and a more compact skull along with'unnatural' coat colors and patterns like light silver, timber and piebald (white with patches of color).

Also, they barked and whined for focus, a Behavior restricted to puppyhood in crazy canines, against their national dogs, that maintain the capability to bark to the entirety of the lives (characteristic individuals loved when they understood that these creatures might alert them to an intruder or other threat). The foxes' dentition also shifted, exactly like with all our domestic dogs they had precisely the same amount of teeth because their wild ancestors, but using a more compact jaw, a few of the teeth (the third and second premolars) must sit down in an angle concerning the other people. Probably the very unique attribute that demonstrated in those domesticated foxes has been a 2nd annual heat cycle, precisely like in puppies (with the exclusion of this Basenji).

Since the choice procedure (both In dogs and foxes) concentrated on obedience and trainability, and surely not aesthetics, what exactly does jacket color have to do with those traits? It ends up that genes which code for hydration can also be involved in different processes, like the metabolism of hormones, namely dopamine and adrenaline; the primary being a compound released in reaction to pressure, accountable for the fight or flight reaction, and the next being the significant neurotransmitter involved with reward-motivated behaviours. A mutation someplace in those genes caused a diminished adrenergic answer, higher sensitivity to the production of dopamine in addition to a reversal of saliva production, creating the variegated coating patterns observed from both domestic dogs and foxes.

Even Though wolves and dogs belong to the very same species, it's paedomorphism which produces dogs, thus domesticable and predators maybe not. From the domestic pet, limbic system growth is diminished, leading to a 20 percent drop in proportion in dogs in contrast to their lupine relatives. A bigger limbic system usually means an attenuation of competitive and fearful answers. Docility and also the lack of fear involving individuals are traits which play a massive part in the mutual achievement of their human-dog relationship.

Virtually All the Traits we find desired in our pet puppies are juvenile wolf traits: being friendly, extroverted, reliant creatures is precisely what makes dogs simple to create a bond with. In ways, dogs could be considered teenager wolves within their behaviour (barking, whining, and dependency on civic amounts for crucial tools and attachment.) in addition to some physical characteristics, like a pendant or semi-erect ears and a shorter, broader snout, as observed in several dog breeds.

Coppinger and Coppinger were the very first to try to set dog breeds according to their behavioural adulthood concerning wolf growth, hypothesizing that particular facial characteristics that liken adult puppies into wolf pups of specific ages were educating of the maturity level. The younger the puppy, the dog, looks, the longer paedomorphic he's. And though the statement mentioned above is a bit too blunt, it's correct that many strains do resemble (so much as snout form and ear carriage) a wolf puppy at the same level of developmental maturity. For example, mountain puppies or mastiffs, like the Rottweiler, using a comparatively short, broad snout and ring ears possess a similar profile to that of two to three-week-old wolf puppy. They're one of the more lively and wholesome strains, believed "perennial dogs". Not too much off, we've got many retrievers, like the Golden Retriever and the Labrador Retriever, together with several hounds, like the Beagle. The somewhat sweeter snout and ring ears might appear to indicate the similarity to a slightly older wolf puppy; those puppies are generally more orally fixated compared to other strains and revel in chewing and playing things, actually at a few weeks old is if wolf pups begin to venture from their den and research. Progressing further, we've got the Collies, using their semi-erect ears and much more gracile snout they resemble wolf pups of approximately a few months old, using their strong urge to chase. Ultimately, we've got many Nordic strains, shepherds along with sighthounds, all owning decidedly more lupine attributes: upright ears and long, pointed snout. They resemble wolf pups between ten and six months old, with a slowly increasing victim drive.

Despite a specific correlation Between maturity and appearance, the institution is not perfect. There are lots of strains which have characteristics not found in wolf pups, as a result of expanding popularity of choosing for bodily traits instead of temperamental ones along with also a preference for hyper types, in different words critters possessing exaggerated physical characteristics which aren't just futile, but generally detrimental (short or deviated limbs, bulging eyes, brachycephaly, etc..) .), the aforementioned proposed version is growing more and more unreliable, and trying to deduce somebody's character by assessing snout allometry (the association between shape and size) and ear carriage is a suspect at best.

Although our Domestic dogs are a far cry from their wolf relatives, so particular wild adult behaviours still linger inside their ethogram, however with bits missing or with no exact end. The most obvious example of this is sometimes observed in dogs that are parasitic. These creatures go through each of the first phases of searching: they stem and chase their prey, so a few even stings their heels. However, there's not any killing or ingestion of the possessions they're herding. Although this engine design is quite helpful for the people working with these puppies, it's utterly useless to the puppies; it's only self-remunerative: that the reward can be found in the behaviour itself (herding), instead of attaining a particular ending (insatiable appetite).

Learning And play behaviours are juvenile characteristics which decrease as a person ages. Hence, it's been hypothesized that humans are Paedomorphy, keeping a heightened ability to find out beyond adolescence and Well into maturity. And not just people, It's Been hypothesized that All domestic creatures are paedomorphic variations of the wild ancestors. It stands to reason, then, that choice for juvenile traits (friendliness, reliance on public figures.) will return a Person having a high capacity to learn much as an adult, a characteristic Humans would search for in the creatures that function alongside them.

DEALING WITH DOG AGGRESSION

Dog aggression can be an extremely complicated thing for the typical dog owner to manage. Just once you've worked out which sort of aggressive behaviour your pet is introducing will likely be able to locate a remedy and place a plan in place to repair the issue and revel in the business of your pet.

It should go without saying that the proprietors of aggressive dogs must NOT use physical punishment because of the response. Typically, this kind of plan will only ever create the aggression issue worse. Punishing dominance, territorial, anxiety established, diverted, possessive, or even protective pet aggression will only elicit much more cerebral aggression and may lead to acute strikes and biting episodes. This may also set your pet under much more anxiety, and we know that excessive anxiety as in people will finish your pet's life.

Dogs with aggression issues need comprehension, NOT Additional torture. Since the puppy's owner, the faster you learn precisely what's bothering your puppy, the more precise his therapy is going to be, and the earlier he is going to have the ability to regain.

Handling dog aggression may be handled efficiently and immediately provided you understand precisely what you're doing. This is quite significant inexperienced or dumb pet owners who try to fix aggressive puppy behaviour are not just there lifestyle but also the lifestyles of family members along with the general public and of course of their pet. It's crucially important that as a responsible pet owner, you do your homework dog psychology and communicating, and also the avoidance and healing dog aggression issues. Sometimes avoidance of the issue supporting the aggression may be the remedy.

It's worth repeating that you MUST KNOW WHAT YOU'RE DOING if you would like to take care of aggressive behaviour yourself. You have to have the ability to work out precisely why your pet is acting in an aggressive fashion, and require rapid, efficient actions to take care of it. You aren't going to get very much adjusting the behaviour by yelling and yelling at your very best buddy if he behaves in a specific way, several kinds of aggression will probably call for unique approaches. Frequently aggressive behaviour is just a symptom of some other problem your pet has that will have to get diagnosed and treated so.

The guideline is that if you're in any doubt on why your pet is acting aggressively, or the way you're able to prevent the aggressive behaviour speak to your furry friend and find the particulars of an expert that will manage assist you to diagnose the difficulties behind your pet behaviour and help you place a training plan rather than return your pet to his regular behaviour.

Having a puppy ought to be a mutually beneficial connection, which explains the reason why there are an estimated 100 million dog owners Net, so remember you aren't alone and like the rest of us Pet owners that you love your dog just like that he loves you.

DOG SEPARATION ANXIETY

Separation anxiety is a problem that lots of dogs encounter when left at home or in a less comfortable location. It's a normal reaction to get a puppy to become bonded with its mother and littermates, and if he leaves the clutter, this bond will move to the proprietor. This is usually a healthy connection and creates a relationship between a puppy and owner. It's merely a problem once the dog gets overly determined by its proprietor and behavioural issues are made.

Separation anxiety is often evidenced by urinating and defecating in the home by a generally house-trained puppy, destruction of furniture and other things such as beds, flooring, doors and furniture, barking, whining, hyperactivity and crying. The dog might also look depressed, though it's imperative to keep in mind that each one these traits may have different causes, both the medical and emotional, thus a checkup in the vets is the very first plan of action. Separation anxiety is most likely the offender if the behaviour occurs shortly after the death of the proprietor and in the event the dog provides a hyperactive, protracted greeting as soon as the owner returns.

Particular breeds of dogs tend to be more reliant and are far more vulnerable to separation anxiety, but so too are puppies that have experienced traumatic events in their past which have encouraged a heightened attachment when they eventually locate a husband. Puppies which were removed from their mother too early and dogs or dogs who have invested some time in pet stores or animal shelters are more vulnerable to distress when left alone with their proprietor. Changes in lifestyle and routine such as unexpectedly working fulltime and being outside daily or strange lack of a relative because of death, divorce or illness may upset puppies that typically show no symptoms of separation anxiety.

A dog suffering from separation anxiety will exhibit his very own distinct behavioural issues - some will create one difficulty although some are going to show several, sometimes start the stress cycle while the proprietor remains in the home in expectation of him departing. A puppy which follows its owner from room to room, whines and whimpers, shakes and usually seems desperate as the owner must leave home is very frequently beginning its occurrence of stress. This is the point where an operator can start to re-train their puppy to respond differently to their death.

A method called "planned departure" has established to be quite powerful and is a lot more useful than just adjusting the behaviour, as it addresses the reason for the issue. The notion is to mould your dog's response by building a string of brief departures. Since the nervous reaction always happens very soon after the owner leaves the premises, the puppy is abandoned for just a couple of minutes (or maybe seconds to begin with) to make sure he returns until the puppy gets frenzied. The proprietor must leave home quietly and peacefully without talking to the puppy or giving him focus and ought not to permit the puppy to display protracted compliments on his return merely ignoring the behaviour and turning off will slowly dissuade this. The projected departures ought to be quite gradually increased in duration, not remaining far long enough to allow your puppy to become bloated or bloated. It takes the time to break old habits and patience will be essential, but this procedure will gradually do the job. When the puppy is untroubled through a half minute passing, the duration of time can be raised by larger increments.

If this technique is taking a very long time and will be showing little indication of being Successful, the proprietor can increase the potency by systematically Blowing off the puppy around your home for some time around three months. The Puppy won't suffer from that point, nor will the bond between owner and dog Be diminished, but the puppy will surely be confused initially, mainly If he is used to lots of attention. It may help a dependent, nervous Dog locate a more calm, more distinct presence which will alleviate Phases of being alone at the house.

DOG BEHAVIOUR PROBLEMS

Dog behaviour issues are for the central part, made by people. The standard treatment will be improper and completely confuses the puppy. This is not uncommon in so-called expert dog trainers and veterinarians alike.

Dog Training methods typically completely lack knowledge about where the puppy is coming out of. They are frequently unpleasant, frightening or even downright unkind. Veterinary therapy is a little higher, with the debut of pet antidepressant drugs to increase the multitude of toxic medicine that suppresses instead of regretting.

Without comprehending the puppy and why he's acting the way he's, you don't have any possibility of rectifying the circumstance. In reality, it's very likely to worsen.

To give you an example, my neighbour brought home a brand new pup some weeks past. He's become a massive dog. He's the only puppy. They're out at work daily. I guess he's intended to be a dog.

This puppy is quite lonely. He's smart and has found the way to escape. He does not go far. So far as my location. To pay a visit to my puppies.

To begin with, he had been pleased to attach through the weapon. But he is young and busy. He immediately learned how to leap on the fence.

My puppies thoroughly enjoyed their time rushing around at full rate, taking it in turns out to pursue each other.

When his people found this, they cried. They chastised him when he was coming to them he was coming home. This sets up yet another difficulty in his thoughts - do not visit them when called since they are very likely to be mad.

I proposed to them that he's lonely so that as they're out in the office every single day, they ought to have another puppy. Dogs are pack animals and do not fare well by themselves. They did not like this thought. Instead, they've restrained him so that he could no more escape.

Dog Behavior problems develop due to these essential misunderstandings. Nowadays he is controlled, when he wants to race about, find out in lifestyle, stretch his legs, then thankfully engage with other individuals. He's lonely, even when he wants a bunch, of at least another dog, a person or other creature equivalent to him.

Psychologically, he's very likely to go slowly mad if he's so disposed. Or he is maybe depressed if this is in their character. Perhaps he'll become frustrated. Or mad. This may result in aggression.

And all because people look at animals by using their limited senses. Dogs aren't people. Dogs are dogs also want their fundamental canine needs fulfilled.

The massive majority of dog behaviour problems stem from the misunderstanding of a puppy's very basic demands.

Of course, they want delicious food. They want refuge. They want to exercise. They want your love. However, they also want one to know precisely where they come out. They desperately require the interaction of additional pack animals - additional puppies, you or some other creature who will interact together.

With this, you can expect your puppy to develop severe emotional issues. These puppies are subsequently invariably murdered since they're deemed dangerous to maintain within individual society. Nevertheless, it was the people who made the issue.

UNDERSTANDING DOGS ABILITIES

If we can teach a puppy to draw and provide the idea of "God" it'd draw God as a dog. Many so-called dog coaches and innumerable owners have a confused perception of what constitutes a puppy and also have expectations far over their real ability.

Some people today think their pets can comprehend complicated thought patterns, and also understand our ethical and moral codes; they presume that a dog's level of comprehension is on a level with our own. Dogs operate on driveway degrees and instinct. It's crucial to remember they can't understand the complicated thought processes that attract us to understand human emotions, speech and behaviour.

There's a clear title for this particular Anthropomorphism: The keyword of anthropomorphism is "to assign aggression or thought patterns into objects or animals, that are not capable of accomplishing such measurements". This is similar to describing a vine climbs the tree to find a better opinion.

Anthropomorphism is just one of the principal motives we locate huge trouble communicating effectively together using our pets. So why is it that we take action? People find it a lot easier to link to a thing when they view their emotions and thought patterns to the activities of the animals.

Employing the vine case, this can be an illustration of projection. Projection is a mental phenomenon where one jobs their feelings upon other people, creatures, or objects. This is beneficial in everyday life because it takes the guesswork from fact. Rather than always considering why something is because it can be, you place it in context with the way you believe and your daily life.

Dogs are capable of connecting ideas; however, are incapable of linking activities which are split by time. If for instance, a dog makes a mess throughout your absence there's not any purpose in telling off the dog or rubbing its nose into it, which in my mind is dimmed, you would not rub a kid's nose is a soiled nappy? As well as if you did precisely what instruction procedure would the kid get?

The puppy's mind Can't link the activity with any Passage of time. So many men and women say, "He understands he's done wrong" or even "He appears as guilty as hell". No, he does not he seems submissive since he will read your body language and knows you're annoyed, but not the reason why. Their brains aren't invented to feel guilty because we perceive it.

A dog's mind is a lot more compact than a people, particularly in the top region of the brain known as the cerebrum - the section of the brain related to intellectual functions like memory, speech, comprehension, and plausible and psychological thought.

Dogs Can't understand human language. It's a lot more essential to utilize sound routines, intonation, facial and body language as a communicating. A dog wants to please, and learning ought to be based on positive reinforcement. We ought to be mindful that a sizable portion of your dog's mind is occupied with neurological action, especially the interpretation of odour.

Instinct?

Dogs instinct plays an essential part, and frequently, it isn't easy to know why a lot of dog owners can't distinguish between instinct and intellect. Intuition is an impulse from within.

Instinct creates a dog to behave in specific ways and doesn't have a link with intelligence.

Dogs first instinct is to endure when a puppy is born that he squirms about till he discovers out a teat and then dismisses it. This doesn't demand a learning process; it's purely instinctual. The maternal instinct informs the female to wash up the foetal membrane, also at the first 3 or 4 months to also consume the puppy's faeces if wild creatures smell them to kill the pups.

We all know that no more predators are Likely to Assault the mess but try explaining that to your mother? She's not educated these activities, and she's not seen yet another female take action. It's instinct. Most instincts offer delight to the puppy, and also since it associates the actions with joy, the urge grows more powerful with use.

Here is the cornerstone of training to exploit your pet's Instincts and form it has behaviour patterns, so it is okay to that which people perceive as our needs.

Instinct could be strengthened, weakened or may be distracted. But whenever an ability isn't within the very first place, it cannot be inserted, and it can't be removed. It may lie dormant, but once acquired, it may not be diminished. A puppy with an obsession with pursuing cyclists could be controlled by forming its behaviour, obedience instruction and by providing alternate outlets for it is energy.

Precisely like a puppy is fixed the initial Time he chases a different dog or even a jogger it might give up the thought, but if it's permitted to chase joggers or puppies, then that instinct gets much more powerful and can become an issue behaviour that's hard or perhaps impossible to fix.

Fundamental Training

To begin to instruct your puppy your language, you want to blend the words using an act that reveals the dog exactly what you need, and a few reinforcements - both negative or positive. Say your dog's name. Is it true that the dog reacts (look in you, wag his tail, then proceed toward you)?) Your puppy must ALWAYS have a pleasant experience when he finds his title NEVER unpleasant.

Some People today make a brand new "Bad Dog" title to use for all those terrible pet occasions. To instruct the dog his title, place your puppy near touch, preferably onto a leash so that he does not move off. Say that the puppies name and provide his strap or ear with a tug toward you, or transfer his muzzle on your direction. After the dog looks on your way, instantly utilize your "Good Dog" compliments and voice and stroke your puppy in your head or torso and Begin by giving your pet a treat

Exercise this before looking in the occurs with no tug or cure, continue to exercise for your dog's whole life! It strengthens the communication connection between the dog and the owner.

Educate different words in precisely the same manner. Straightforward one-word commands work. Say your dog's name (to receive his attention - recall that communicating connection!), follow a control, then SHOW him what you desire. PRAISE IMMEDIATELY whenever the activity is finished - even if you MADE him do it! Finally, your puppy will learn how to respond to the control without needing to be revealed, but you should never neglect to praise

Getting your point over

Occasionally words Aren't enough when communication with a puppy. Since dogs need to learn what every term means, each of the additional "additional" words is only a lot of"Blah, Blah" into them! Bear in mind that the Gary Larson cartoon that reveals an owner scolding his puppy, Ginger, then shows precisely what the dog hears "Ginger, blah, blah, blah, Ginger, blah..."

The word NO is used much too frequently and means very little into your puppy, and it's far better to utilize specific terms. Keep them brief, do not use words such as "sit ", it may confuse Use with sit down based on what you would like to convey.

CHAPTER FOUR:
TRAINING PUPPIES NOT TO BITE

It may be a puzzle to why dogs bite a lot when they're young. It's a combination of numerous explanations. It's a relief from back pain, a means of investigating the world about them, a reply to some organic identification instinct, and a mechanism to shield themselves if they're unintentionally hurt. Biting can fulfil diverse needs - it alleviates aching teeth, provides advice concerning the pet's environment and provides them with a self-defence mechanism. As there are many reasons why a dog is biting, there is a range of means by which in which you can train your pet never to bite. Below are a few suggestions on training your pet to quit biting individuals and property.

If your pet is biting since its teeth are all Coming, and it requires to ease the pain and strain on its teeth, you may see it always gnawing at all it could find, such as your precious furniture. To prevent this, you ought to receive your pet a distinctive dental toy. These are in many of various shapes and dimensions but are all designed especially to relieve the pain felt throughout your teething and will continue to keep your pet from biting things it should not be.

Significantly though, You Have to impress your pup out of a young age, it is never okay to bite a person. It's crucial to train a dog to tell them when it's been too severe and can be damaging you. Give the pup a stern and business' no' every time it bites someone and eliminate the hands without jerking. You then need to leave or dismiss the puppy for some time. This may signify that the pup will eventually join biting with missing out on the play and certainly will come to realise it is improper behaviour.

You must be entirely consistent in the way you train your dog to bite. The pup won't ever learn unless they're given the same answer every time and from each individual, they perform. Dogs are creatures of habit and may only ever understand through repetition. Finally, the negative relationships will develop between biting rather than liking themselves, and they'll quit doing this. On the flip side, should they get another response every time, as an instance, somebody jerking away their hand, or hitting on the puppy, or perhaps continuing to perform since it did not hurt that way, the dog will get confused regarding what's okay, and the message won't move in.

In Addition to negative reinforcement Using punishments for poor behaviour, it's also wise to supply positive Reinforcements in the shape of rewards and treats for proper action. If Your pet licks you through play instead of biting, pet and provide them with affection and love, shortly they will understand This is the Right means to perform. Equally, both consistency and reproduction are crucial to making sure the client sticks. Should you adhere to these principles, you and your puppy is going to have far more joyful play period, and Your pet will probably be well trained not to bite your prized furniture.

A brand-new puppy is a supply of pure joy and pleasure in a household. That is till the pup begins to snack! Small kids get fearful, and parents are very frustrated. In the end, this little puppy will become a cherished family pet. How do they bond with the pet when it bites?

First of all, you want to comprehend why a pup bites. By nature, dogs do not bite from spite or meanness. To get a pup, biting can be a means to play. This is the way they collaborated with their littermates. A dog sees biting as part of the social setup. Once people understand the way the puppy functions, it's far less challenging to take the biting and also to assist the pup to learn how to break up the habit.

If you've got the opportunity to observe your pup using his littermates, it can allow you to realise how to socialize with your pet. If that is not possible, the following few tips can help you educate your pet.

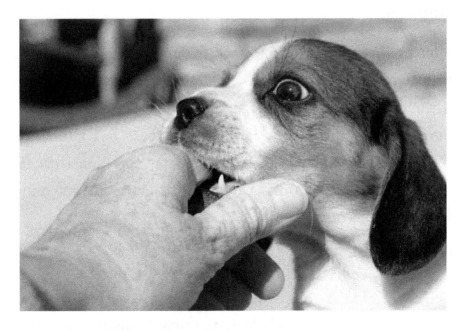

Make Noise

If your dog bites among the littermates into the point of concern, another puppy will yelp. Instantly the puppy will quit biting. In the event you do the very same, the puppy will stop biting you also. Educate other relatives to yelp or create a loud sound once the puppy bites it's going to start to learn this is unacceptable behaviour.

Supply Toys

Much like babies, dogs like to chew things. It is helpful to build up their jaw muscles also operates on their teeth. Supplying chew toys for your dog won't just help stop them from scratching your household, it is also going to save your furniture and shoes!

Withdraw

Puppies are incredibly social creatures, and they like to perform with and be around people. If you stop playing with your puppy when he bites will get the message, it is improper behaviour. On the reverse side, because puppies want to please, he'll attempt to act in a fashion which leads to one to commend him. Thus, be sure that you give your dog a great deal of praise and attention when he's behaving correctly.

Consistency

The most crucial thing that you want to bear in mind is consistency. The puppy will learn the right behaviour quicker if everybody in the household is constant in training. Teach small kids what to do in case the dog nips or snacks. Do training that the puppy a family event and each person will rejoice if the puppy makes progress!

Like small kids, Dogs require patience. Do not expect him to block the behaviour immediately. These things need some time and tender reminding. With continuous reminding and diligence in training, it's possible to aid your pet stop biting and eventually become a Lifelong buddy.

CHAPTER FIVE:
DOG FOOD AND NUTRITION

WHY YOUR PUPPY ISN'T EATING & WHAT TO DO

Dog nutrition plays a massive part in your pet's development and future excellent health. Rather than eating, he will create specific nutrition-related issues in the future. While perhaps not eating for a brief period isn't likely to trigger any long-term troubles, it is vital to be sure that it doesn't survive over a couple of days. Here is what you could do now.

What you may think, dogs do not get tired with their meals. They quit eating for any range of different reasons, such as anxiety, too much action in their dining room, and fresh environment. There is also the prospect of sickness; however, before searching for vet assistance, give it a couple of days to determine whether your puppy starts eating.

A puppy does a lot of the growth from the very first year; therefore, any dog nourishment issues have to be addressed immediately. Your pet's nutrition won't endure if he does not eat for a couple of days, but when his refusal to consume stays, it might endanger his proper expansion.

Whenever your puppy arrives in your house, he will be somewhat dizzy, confused, and stressed since he had been lately removed from his mom and sisters. Dogs are social animals; therefore, this separation could be painful to your young pup. By ensuring that he gets a great deal of attention from the loved ones and can be introduced to and approved by other household pets, so you will allow him to correct more rapidly.

When he quits eating, the worst thing you could do is to hand, as tempting as this is. This may cause a behaviour you do not wish to tackle in the future. The only time you'd give is when your veterinarian suggests it. Otherwise, you want to feed him in a regularly scheduled period daily. If he does not eat the meals in 15 minutes, remove it and then leave just water. Place his food down in his next routine feeding.

You will Probably feel somewhat guilty if your pet is not eating due to the possible problems it may cause. There is not much to be worried about seeing dog nutrition so long as the deficiency of food ingestion is short term. He'll have enough reserves to keep him healthy for a brief time. Nevertheless, you are going to want to look at potential causes of the consumption issues to reevaluate the delay in his obtaining proper nutrition.

Listed below are several things that you can do.

If your pet has nausea, keep tabs on him to determine precisely how awful it is. When it's severe or if it does not cease after the first day, then take your pet to the vet fast as dehydration can develop into a genuine danger to your pet's health.

Consistently put his water and food at the same spot to prevent disruptions in his behaviour. Dogs such as firmness, and transferring his pot around won't help.

Prevent feeding him table scraps since this may disturb his digestive tract and result in specific behaviour problems in the future.

Make sure his dining room is silent during feeding intervals. It is problematic for a pup to centre on eating when children are running around vacuums are operating, and individuals are walking back and forth.

If other pets in the family are demonstrating aggression, aggression, or jealousy from the new pup, keep them from his eating place until he has completed his meals. Nothing may endanger your pet's nutrition intake quicker than creatures hoping to strike him or her take his meals while he is eating.

Once you've ensured his dining space is free from distractions and disruptions, and when he is not eating after a couple of days, take him to a vet. Specific preventable ailments can hinder his urge to consume. Worms are only one typical issue which may be treated easily and quickly.

Worms left untreated could cause your puppy to endure from more severe dog nutrition problems because rats devour the meals before your puppy digests it and also absorbs its nutrient value. If left untreated, worms may cause more significant issues to your pet. The earlier the problem is treated, the earlier your puppy will recuperate and start eating.

A dog's growth rate and long-term wellbeing are affected by his food consumption. Puppies use their nutrient intake faster throughout the formula weeks and months when they perform throughout maturity. It follows they need more supplements to fulfil with the body's growing demands.

Throughout his first calendar year, nourish him a fantastic quality industrial food which was specially formulated to satisfy the nutritional requirements of your growing puppy. By following these simple steps, you can ensure that the pet develops Strong and healthy. It is about making sure that he gets excellent dog Nourishment directly from the beginning.

DOG NUTRITION

Nutrient requirements for puppies have been printed by the National Research Council of the National Academies (NRC) and the Association of American Feed Control Officials (AAFCO). Requirements for suitable dog nourishment are the proportions of those 6 organic elements of meals to fulfil a pet's daily allowance: protein, fat, carbs, minerals, vitamins and water.

For great puppy nutrition, protein must include 21-26 percent of the meals. The distinction between lively, low-active, lite and pup foods would be that the proportion of protein. Proteins are crucial in the right maturation of bone, bone, blood, cells, hormones and enzymes, and also for the appropriate use of the immune system.

The protein component is your most expensive element. The origin of the protein is crucial. There are 22 amino acids which make up proteins, and 10 are crucial for everyday dog nourishment.

Meat protein is nearest to human wellbeing!

The origin of this protein influences its quality. Meat protein is nearest to human wellbeing. Animal protein could be some part which includes protein, for example, skin, hoofs, lips and hair; therefore, it's frequently not digestible. Reduced digestibility of protein usually means that a decrease volume of nourishment available to your dog for the development and maintenance of cells. Pick foods with 2 creature sources of protein in the first five ingredients recorded. Best sources are entire legumes or single-source legumes (i.e. poultry meal versus salmon meal). Steak or grain protein (soy, meat by-products, crude protein, and whatever using "gluten") is frequently unusable protein which could strain the kidneys. Low-quality ingredients aren't absorbed well and may create mosquito. Normally, high-quality protein sources possess greater digestibility and greater price.

Much better quality merchandise is significantly more cost-effective as you get far better dog nourishment for your dollar invested.

Carbohydrates should include 42 percent of meals and contain rice, sausage, cheese, corn, wheat and barley. Both carbs and fats are resources of energy. Fibre is a vitamin which assists in nutrient absorption, gut regulation, and also controlling caloric consumption by supplying satiety. However, fibre isn't a fantastic supply of energy.

In great dog nutrition, usable fats should include 15-20 percent of meals. Fats are vital to puppies with high energy requirements since they provide double the power per gram than protein or carbohydrates. Usable fats comprise poultry fat, sunflower/canola oil, fish oil, and lactose-free dairy product. Tallow fat is unusable. Fats supply palatability of meals and therefore are necessary for even-tempered energy levels, healthful coat and skin, digestion, and also steady body temperature.

A balanced diet is your ideal approach to fix nutrient consumption.

In good dog nutrition, vitamins and minerals, each comprise approximately 1 percent of meals. Nerves, muscles cells require nutritional supplements, which interact to generate chemical enzymes. Too much of a couple of nutritional supplements, like in ellagic acid, can adversely impact others. Even though the number of vitamins needed is modest, they're required for a large number of biochemical purposes. Again, a balanced diet, with no indiscriminate supplementation, would be your ideal approach. Water has become the most crucial element and the simplest to feed properly. Be positive that clean, freshwater is available constantly.

Generic brands may incorporate meat from dead, dying, diseased, or sterile animals, and fats that are senile.

Dog Food is categorized into 3 classes based on calibre. Generic brands may consist of 4-D beef from dead, dying, diseased or decaying creatures, and fats that are senile. Premium food is created from high levels of beef and a greater amount of fats that are usable. Holistic feed, or even homemade diet, also comprises human grade meats, digestible carbs along with also a grain carbohydrate mixture of high quality. It's frequently hormone-free and calorie-loaded so less majority must fulfil dog nutrition instructions. Homemade dog nutrition is growing ever more popular, particularly in light of pet food recalls because of poisonous raw ingredients in China. But, homemade diet ought to be ready in close consultation with your vet to guarantee balanced puppy nutrition.

Now that you know the differences, for a genuine protector, feed your puppy an excellent diet.

Also, look to steer clear of synthetic preservatives (BHA, BHT, ethoxyquin), artificial colors and additives (corn syrup, sucrose, ammoniated glycyrrhizin).

Inappropriate pet nutrition, Diet has to reflect age, weight, activity level, in addition to potential Medication factors. Diet treatment is readily available for heart Ailments, kidney problems, bladder ailments, food allergies and acute obesity. Your pet's health and endurance depend considerably on the quality of nourishment it receives.

Dogs, The same as everybody, have particular nutrient requirements. Dogs lack the capability to convey their issues; therefore, it is up to their own owners to find out how healthy they may be. Diet directly impacts your pet's coat and skin, weight, skill level, and digestive function. Diet, environmental toxins, pharmaceuticals and stress all play a role in the health of companion animals. Dog nourishment affects overall wellbeing, including coat and skin condition.

Feeding your pet can be performed in three distinct ways: pet food bought at the grocery store, pet food produced in the home or even a blend of both. Should you choose to buy commercial pet food, I'd suggest doing some reading about it, even in a previous couple of years several commercial pet foods have needed to be recalled because of contaminants which are observed in pet food. Many pet owners are choosing holistic pet foods, within the commercially available pet foods, in an attempt to present their dogs into a much healthier, more balanced diet plan. Dog foods should contain little if any fillers in any way, but the majority of them do this that your really not giving your pet the appropriate diet it ought to be healthful. Many recipes are located on the web for pet foods you'll be able to create out of your property.

Irrespective of everything you choose to feed your pet, it's crucial to make sure your pet isn't receiving access to food all of the time. This may cause obesity, which may cause much different disorder for the furry friend. Free-feeding is likewise quite beneficial for the practice of meal intervals in dogs and leaving out food in warm summer months may bring fleas, flies and other insects from the woodwork. It's suggested your pet is on an eating program and keep in mind to only offer the sum prescribed by your veterinarian, an excessive amount of food may also make obesity. Bear in mind; dogs are scavengers; a complete jar is often a cause for pleading or surfing behaviour and doesn't signify your dog is hungry.

Feeding your pet table scraps may Also be a lousy training and nourishment habit. Your pet will beg although you eat your own dinner, which may be embarrassing for visitors but also human fats, and meals aren't always great for your dog since they are for you personally. I suggest feeding your loved ones while your puppy eats his meals in a different area. In this manner, he will not feel left out.

Dogs possess shorter digestive tracts than individuals, and bigger chunks may upset your puppies' gut. Your pet requires a well-balanced daily diet, high in protein (that is not saved as fat) and fat and low in carbohydrate. Nutrition is not necessarily about diet. Fantastic nutrition contributes to great health and thus do lots of different items, like exercise, maintaining down its weight (through good nutrition and regular exercise) maintaining its teeth clear (alongside obesity, periodontal disease will be one most commonly found in your vet's office) taking it into the vet for routine check-ups being observant about symptoms which may suggest a health issue and receiving prompt and proper veterinary care (information below).

You may also wish to think about alternative remedies for any illness or allergies your pet has. These could consist of nutrition, acupuncture, herbs, massage, and massage, in addition to conventional medications. These choices are natural and better for the dog's own body than chemical medications and don't have any side effects in any way. As more individuals understand the significance of nourishment for their health, they are beginning to consider what is inside their pet's food bowl too. Maximum nutrition dog foods may do a great deal for your pet's wellbeing by enhancing its physical appearance, skill level and overall condition of health.

Learn what you need to be feeding your pet at every point Of its own life. By knowing what dogs eat from the wild, you may Learn valuable hints regarding what you ought to be feeding your national puppy. The amount to which contemporary dogs undergo ailing health reflects the Degree to which they're exposed to inappropriate procedures Of exercising and feeding. If your puppy consistently leaves some meals in the bowl, you're most likely consuming an excessive amount of food. Keep your pet's nutrition, diet, food, and eating customs, and he/she will dwell a happy Life together with you and your nearest and dearest.

NEVER GIVE FOOD SCRAPS TO YOUR DOG

Dogs' Digestive system is certainly similar to ours, so only using this as a beginning point, it might be wise to think dog nutrition cannot be exactly the exact same. We season our foods into our preferences and desires, employing all sorts of condiments, spices and all conceivable to make them elegant and great for us, however, these very same spices and other ingredients we all place in our food may cause enormous damage to our pet's gastrointestinal tract, causing example, bad breath, gas and loose stools, and among other possessions. Why wreak distress to some being we state we adore?

If in addition, we think about the fact that providing our puppies with the additional calories that come out of greasy acids scraps will surely create weight reduction, it's very important to keep in mind that obese dogs are constantly at a higher chance of introducing complications like diabetes, cardiovascular disease and other undesirable illnesses like pancreatitis. Their healthful diets should be determined by high protein intake, though many pet foods also incorporate veggies today.

Many pet owners aren't Knowledgeable about the truth that there are lots of foods they ought to never nourish for their dogs, like vanilla and chocolate goods. We typically utilize onions to generate our meals taste better; however, these may be hazardous to the puppy, for example, powder type. When we condiment our meals with blossoms and give our pet scraps comprising it, what could be anticipated?

We may face problems sometimes digesting certain foods, and puppies aren't distinct in that way. They do not understand that, so in the event that you donate sugar or corn, you may expect them to be hard on your pet's digestive tract. This also contains lunch, sausage meats and other condiments which are high in sugar content.

We're used to believing dogs love bones, And that's accurate, however, if we provide them meat products which include bones inside them, these may crack and puncture the throat, intestines or stomach. This occurs to people also, so keep it in mind. Should they obstruct the digestive pathway, constipation might be the outcome. Oh, yes, licking at the bone is most likely an extremely rewarding experience for your puppy, but should be the ending of it. In case the bone begins cracking, that's the opportunity to eliminate it.

Many puppy foods have been prepared for the puppy's digestive system and provide them of the appropriate nutrition they want, but in addition, there are specific recipes you can prepare in your home for the dog which were said to help them not just stay fitter, but also longer lifestyles.

Jumping in the physical to the emotional facet of giving your pet the table scraps even though you're having dinner, remember that in the event you take action, the puppy will translate that as a reward because of his requesting, and that means you'd then must be ready for this behaviour to repeat itself each single time you sit in the dining table. Even though it might appear adorable as I mentioned above, that scene isn't sufficient and shouldn't introduce itself. You've got your own time for supper and they ought to have theirs, aside from one another.

We do work with food as a means to reinforce the behaviour we desire from our puppies, regardless of where we need it to manifest itself (house, neighborhood, displays, etc.). However, this should be utilized when we're training our pet instead of merely because. There are lots of great snacks you may offer your dog when performing so rather than feeding it that which will produce harm, even though yummy.

Recall It's your obligation to select the ideal nutrition for the dogs. If left to these, there isn't any end to the things they find appealing to their flavour without being aware of what the impacts may be.

CHOOSE DOG BONES WISELY

Healthy dog nutrition seems to be a simple goal; however, there are particular foods which you watch. While puppies in the wild have a powerful mood, tamed pets are more prone to the harsh quality of several foods. Knowing which foods to prevent will help stop your pet from unnecessary distress.

Any pet owner knows just how much dogs love bones; however, not all of the bones are helpful for your furry friend.

In terms of pet nutrition, bones may offer excellent sources of protein and specific minerals. Regrettably, there's a negative effect on bones which may be detrimental and even dangerous for your dog. That is why it's important that you're cautious which bones that you enable your puppy to eat.

The worst bones are the ones which are delicate and are inclined to splinter, including bones, lamb bones, chicken bones as well as some other bones which create shards. Boiled bones of any type can get brittle and break away in harmful jagged bits.

These sharp bits can become lodged in your pet's neck or gastrointestinal tract, causing acute pain and discomfort. Left untreated, your pet might die from the congestion and harm the bones may cause. Plus, it can occur very fast.

You will be pleased to know you don't need to invade your dog of their dog nourishment available . It is merely a matter of understanding which bones are most healthy.

If you would like to feed your puppy on bones, then select the thick knucklebones and around bones as you see in beef. Your butcher can offer these bones for you. You will possibly get the cost, which is an excellent bonus taking into consideration the price of pet food.

Bones with meat supply excellent dog nourishment; however, you can raise the value with the addition of different ingredients into your pet's diet - components you may not otherwise think about feeding your pet.

You can spend less on the pricey, specially formulated dog but be sure you are aware that it is a fantastic option. Check the label to ensure that the very first ingredients are entire meat rather than beef additives, corn or alternative item. Bear in mind, the ingredients listed are the maximum content from the bundle. To put it differently, if steak is recorded , you can be certain that there is going to be a fantastic amount of beef within the bag of foods.

Conversely, whether corn or wheat is recorded on top, the meals will probably offer small dog nutrition since it's primary component is filler.

Fresh meat is obviously best, but it has to be cooked to eliminate any harmful germs. Mix it together with grated carrots and soil eggshells to improve the vitamins, calcium and minerals on your pet's diet. Eggshells are high in vitamin E. It's possible to buy eggshells as a nutritional supplement, or just crush these cubes which you toss out following your cook with your morning eggs and bacon.

If You are worried about dog's wellbeing, add these additional actions, and you can be certain your pet will secure the ideal dog nutrition it's possible to supply

DOG NUTRITIONAL SUPPLEMENTS

Dogs Which are correctly fed normally do not demand dog supplements. They get whatever nutrient requirements they have in the pet food which they are fed. You can find dogs which may require dog supplements and all these are dogs who have particular needs. Older dogs might also require some nutritional supplements because their age may be a factor for their own failing health.

Giving your dog the Ideal dog food is Usually sufficient to pay their nutrient requirements. In case you've got a new pup, seek advice from your vet concerning dog supplements or that pet food is much more complete with all the essential minerals and vitamins.

Components of Dog Nutritional Supplements

Calcium And Phosphorous are a number of the vital elements required in dog supplements since these help elderly dogs and young dogs shape and keep bones that are good. Although, these ought to be granted in moderation unless defined from the vet because a lot of both elements aren't god to the dog.

Other dog supplements are Potassium and sodium chlorate. Potassium and sodium are necessary as electrolyte components for the dogs. A lot of them can give rise to a kidney malfunction unless given by your veterinarian don't devote a lot of.

Microelements are necessary for the good functioning of a fantastic metabolism. This is necessary by dogs with issues with excessive weight — zinc results in the absorption of proteins and aids in creating the pet's skin and fur better. Dog supplements with zinc ought to be provided only to dogs which need it because some dog foods currently contain zinc.

Iron is an essential component in pet nutritional supplements as it helps fight anaemia and is necessary for good blood flow and supply. Iodine is also dog supplements since this helps alleviate the bones and thyroid gland. Excessive iodine may lead to hyperthyroidism.

Other pet supplements which can be Useful to possess had been cod liver oil and puppies multi-vitamins. Cod liver oil can help to make the skin and coat of our puppies glistening and healthy although multi-vitamins for puppies provide little doses of all part of vitamins your pet may be lacking.

Self-evident or self Medicating might be a risky practice as there are particular doses which rely on the dimensions and weights of these dogs. Never forget to speak with your vet concerning the appropriateness of vitamins or puppy supplements.

The same as people, dogs, have been influenced by the health risks of Contemporary living. Pollution, poor nutrition, stress and unhealthy lifestyles may result in many different ailments and ailments, which are extremely like those experienced by people.

Nowadays, bodily ailments like diabetes, arthritis, gastrointestinal disorders, liver and kidney problems, skin disorders, obesity, thyroid disorder and other issues are getting increasingly more prevalent from the pet.

Luckily Many, or even most, of those ailments can be avoided by assisting your pet to live a healthy lifestyle. For puppies suffering from Present circumstances, a combination of lifestyle changes and organic Supplements may work miracles!

PROTEINS AND AMINO ACIDS

Dogs can't endure without nourishment in their diets. Dietary protein includes 10 particular amino acids which dogs can't make by themselves. Called key amino acids, they supply the building blocks for several significant biologically active proteins and compounds. Additionally, they contribute the carbon chains necessary to make sugar for energy. High-quality proteins possess a fantastic balance of each critical amino acids. Studies indicate that dogs can tell if their meals lack one amino acid and also will avert this type of meal. Dogs have been known to choose foods which have a lot of protein. Whether that is only a matter of preference or an intricate reaction to their biological requirements of all 10 essential amino acids isn't known. But dogs may live on a vegetarian diet so long as it includes adequate protein and can be supplemented with vitamin D from pet supplements.

FATS AND FATTY ACIDS

Dietary fats, chiefly derived from animal fats as well as also the seed oils of different plants, supply the most concentrated source of energy from your diet. They provide essential fatty acids that can't be contained in the human body and function as carriers such as significant fat-soluble vitamins. Fatty acids play a part in cellular structure and function. Food fats have a tendency to boost the flavour and feel of their pet's food too. Essential fatty acids are required to maintain your pet's coat and skin healthy. Dogs fed ultra-low-fat diets create dry, rough skin and hair lesions which become vulnerable to diseases. Deficiencies at the so-called"omega-3" household of essential fatty acids might be related to eyesight issues and diminished learning ability. Another family of fatty acids known as"omega-6" was proven to have significant physiologic effects within the human body.

CHAPTER SIX:
DOG EXERCISE

IMPORTANT CONSIDERATIONS FOR DOG EXERCISE

A Lot was said concerning the ramifications lack of practice has in puppies, something that I believe very important for many dog owners to understand. Now I want to mention some important tips to consider in another way since the ramifications of them could harm rather than help you puppy, which is precisely the opposite of what any pet owner would desire.

The very first things to consider are the age, breed and size of the puppy. Dogs could not endure exactly the identical quantity of exercise as a teenager dog. You may see they invest a great deal of time throughout the day going, playing and just being inquisitive. However, you'll also see they spend several hours . That means that they understand when to work out and should break, exactly like human infants.

Youthful dogs will, naturally, have a great deal of energy; nonetheless, that doesn't indicate that energy can keep them jumping or running all day . As a matter of fact, various studies have revealed that running and continuous or continuing jogging can damage rather than advantage young puppies because their bones haven't completed the pure development process, nonetheless.

Elderly dogs, just due to the natural path of life, could reveal not as much endurance and energy whilst exercising; therefore, it's necessary always to be attentive to what it reveals it could endure. Many people today are inclined to overlook the ageing procedure in dogs isn't the same as ours, thus in the event, the pet owner doesn't have any notion of their dog's actual age, the info is on the world wide web and may also be readily ascertained by requesting its vet. Do not make the mistake of stressing your pet is exactly what you would like it to be rather than what it is actually as far as age is concerned simply because it seems to be matched to you. Many dog owners really do neglect here and attempt to force their puppies to go on and off when the creature has shown signs of becoming drained.

Little dogs along with short-haired puppies do not want too much exercise as bigger ones, so be certain that you do this. Do not feign to possess your Chihuahua or even Dachshund follow exactly the identical pattern as your Collie or even Labrador Retriever.

When contemplating breeds, the listing should start by putting your pet in the right category or category, in case it happens to function as a pristine one. According to the AKC, there are seven Chief categories:

Sporting Dogs

Hound Dogs

Running Dogs

Terriers

Toys

Herding Dogs

Non-Sporting Dogs

Sporting, Hound, Working and Herding dogs are obviously Designed for endurance and exercise, and a few Terriers have a propensity to function as feisty and energetic creatures. In this last class, do remember to also think about the size of their dog, because Terriers do change a good deal.

Other crucial features to remember when contemplating a workout program to your dog would be the structural or physiological ones. Some examples of them are:

Dogs belonging to Breeds with brief or flat noses such as Pug, French Bulldog, Boxer or Pekingese often have breathing or respiratory difficulties if they're excessively exercised.

Some hounds, known as sighthounds, where Group we could come across the Greyhounds and Whippets, are built for conducting short rather than extended distances.

When we see substantial, strong puppies, such as German Shepherds, Rottweilers or Siberian Huskies, we envision they're ready for anything having to do with a workout, and we're mistaken. Huge dogs are generally prone to particular sinus injuries, to hip dysplasia and arthritis, and therefore a prolonged or continuing exercise plan can harm rather than advantage them.

Additionally, there Are those Breeds that reveal a propensity to bloat. In these, we locate that the narrow-bodied breeds such as German Shepherds, Great Danes and Doberman Pinschers. The key point to keep in mind here is never to take any puppy belonging to the group to exercise it has had its own meal.

Fantastic dog owners are almost always cautious about their pet's health state, which is only one of the most crucial issues to remember while considering dog practice.

A person suffering from a trendy illness or even a heart weakness would not participate in an exercise program without consulting with his doctor? The same is true for dogs. If the pet owner isn't Training certain about his pet's health state, he should have it assessed by its vet and follow her directions concerning what exercise plan to follow along with what things to avoid for your dog to gain rather than be hurt by it.

As exercise Is Essential in Any puppy's life, therefore is the suitable kind of exercise along with the adequate moment. The puppy will practice the exact same based on its own individual needs and requirements.

WHY DOG EXERCISE IS SO IMPORTANT

Small must be mentioned about the demand for adequate puppy exercise - it's vitally important to the puppy as normal exercise is valuable to you personally. Dogs aren't intended to stay inactive and develop fat - a trimming, a well-conditioned puppy will endure much more than an obese one. Normal exercise will offer your pet a toned core which may deal nicely with the proper quantity of body fat and also be in a position to resist disease nicely.

The Key to a dog's health and well-being would be to maintain them all exercise. Fit dogs have a tendency to be more content and alert. In addition, they get much better sleep, also have more energy and also interact much better. By practice, they are going to safeguard from health issues and boredom equally. In addition, it reinforces the bond between you and your furry friend.

Dogs typically enjoy wide-open spaces to operate around. But nowadays, not many families have sufficient space to allow their own dogs to perform with. You have to offer your dog three or more short walks per day, among which has to allow for many minutes of vigorous action. Dogs become idle if they aren't invited to exercise.

Swimming is also an excellent action. It is low-impact and total. This pet exercise is very valuable for dogs that perform along with other competitive sports. It is possible even to incorporate reclaiming games whenever you're swimming with your puppy. Swimming in the shore is a fantastic selection for the warm summertime because it provides him with a fantastic workout without the probability of being overheated. Just make sure you give him clean water following a dip from the shore.

Another enjoyable dog workout is fetching. You are able to instruct your dog to fetch a ball another toy or thing designed especially for dog pulling. It is also possible to try letting your puppy catch a Frisbee - puppies that understand how to bring balls and other things would easily determine what to do using you.

As fun as The dog drill may be, it is highly recommended not to forget things. Quit playing until your puppy becomes tired and exhausted - that is going to keep the puppy exercise intriguing to him. Permit him to break after each exercise session, and so he is going to be anticipating another time he performs you.

While providing them exercise, keep in mind not to allow him to overheat. Avoid the hottest aspect of the evening to perform the workout. Constantly provide an ample source of clean water for your pet, so you are able to avoid dehydration. Be mindful not to allow your puppy to overexert himself as this may result in harm.

Normal exercise is beneficial for you and your pet. You have to include it into his everyday routine - as you know, dogs have regularly been enjoying. His workout regimen should fit nicely on your program, and you ought to stick to it . Remember that if a puppy doesn't have a suitable outlet for his energy, then he might tend to develop into harmful, nervous and even gloomy.

Each Dog breed demands different levels of everyday exercise and activity. Pros say that a few daily exercise and activity is critical to maintaining your pet's physical and psychological health at an optimal level. Deficiency of dog practice will result in obesity, poor muscle tone, and heart issues, joint and bone ailments and can often lead to psychological difficulties, anxiety biting, destructive behaviour, and nervousness.

That Is the reason why a normal exercise regimen is an indispensable part of a puppy's healthy way of life. Appropriate nutrition, dressing and routine visits to your vet will also be just as important to keep your pet healthy and happy. Ideally, a workout program ought to be established whenever your puppy is still a pup and lasted through your pet life. Try to be aware of the qualities of your puppy, to begin with, to establish the ideal exercise program for him.

Offering your pet exercise every day will considerably decrease her risk for accidents and ailments, for example:

Diabetes

Obesity

Heart disorder

Bone and joint ailments

Reduced muscle building

Digestive disorders

Depression

Exercise may also allow your furry friend Buddy to sleep , meaning he will not be awake during the night, making a sound. And additionally, it will improve his immune system by obtaining a proper night's sleep, consequently preventing the beginning of the life-threatening ailments. Another advantage for you and your furry friend is the dog exercise can help build an enduring bond with your pet. Whenever your puppy exercises, you are going to be right there along with your furry friend, setting a bond of confidence. This is particularly vital for saving dogs, timid dogs and puppies only lately embraced.

These kinds of dogs particularly want to establish that bond with you so as to turn into a better-behaved furry friend. Dogs that profit from daily exercise are not as inclined to become more competitive and therefore are more affectionate and faithful since they bond with you through strolling together and enjoying games. Exercise gives your puppy the perfect character, which makes him a loving, faithful dog who is not aggressive toward other dogs and those who he or she succeeds.

The pet owner understands that a daily dog drill Regular is merely part of having a puppy. As Soon as You've welcomed a puppy In your own life, you have to give him sufficient exercise every day to maintain both your pet and you healthy and happy. A correctly exercised dog Will sleep well, suffer from left nervousness when left alone, will soon probably be Less competitive, and is generally happier and more satisfied.

DOG EXERCISE PENS

Selecting to put in a Dog into an own family's lifestyle may be a life-altering choice. Dogs, especially dogs, have a custom of getting over your lifetime! They have to be walked, they have to get cleaned up afterwards, and they'll chew everything.

The majority of the bad behaviour that they exhibit can readily be trained outside and will even fall naturally as they develop from the puppy phase. However, in the meantime that they are just like a storm through your home and house.

Dog Exercise Pens may be a very wise addition to your house when you're considering a dog or a pup. Basically, they're a lightweight mobile structure which has your pet. They are not cages and are open atmosphere, but you ought to restrict their time at there - no puppy needs to be eternally caged or limited.

Consider this; you still have a brand-new pup. That's chewing on your pricey couch every single time you leave the space. As opposed to awaiting your practice to kick and suppress the behaviour, putting him at a Dog Exercise Pen as you are not with him gives him lots of space to manoeuvre around, but ceases the path of devastation in its tracks.

This can also be very helpful during bathroom training. Putting a Dog Exercise Pen within a readily cleanable location (more tiles or despite paper on the floor) will prevent your puppy from creating a mess in your carpeting. This will also aid in preparing your dog to get it done company in 1 place instead of anywhere and anyplace!

Dog Exercise Pens may additionally give toddlers a feeling of land and possession; it is their distance. This can allow you to avoid the common situation in which the puppy becomes the ruler of the home rather than you! Since Cesar Milan, among the world's leading authorities on dog behaviour, says, again and again, it is extremely imperative that you're the dominant person on your connection. This does not mean developing a submissive puppy; it merely suggests that you have to be regarded as the one accountable. Giving your pet, it's own little parcel of land will aid with this.

Another massive advantage can be if you've got friends encounter which has a natural fear of dogs. It is quite common regrettably and can usually be overcome Through controlled discussion. Getting Your new dog at a dog exercise Pen, to begin with, enables your customers to meet them without fear Which can help them bond with no putting them available in an area with what they may find as an unpredictable creature.

Dog Exercise pens usually aren't frequently utilized simply to educate pets. There are instances when people need a place where their beloved pet is going to be shielded, a place where the puppy will become quite a little sunlight and ease himself. The exercise pencil supplies an area where your puppy could be outside and romp with no owner fretting about him running to traffic as well as getting lost.

However, most dogs Will Need to have out for Walks on a regular basis, however, and also the exercise pen shouldn't be an alternative for actual exercise. Additionally, most pet owners are going to profit from a regular walk around the block also.

A pen is a great option for dogs when they're small dogs. This is a great spot to prepare young dogs to relieve themselves outside in the yard instead of indoors on the ground or floor. There are a number of sorts of pens that can be found in the industry. They are available in assorted sizes, colors, layouts and costs, and several snaps together in order that they may be easily taken aside and put off when not used.

Individuals who own a sizable lawn can really purchase 2 pens and unite them with each other to create an extra-large play area. The pencil alone should have no uncovered screws or wires which can injure or reduce the puppy.

The greater quality dog pen Include an entrance door so that the pet owner doesn't need to grow into and from the exercise pen. The entry door must also have a lock to the exterior. Hence the dog does not open it and runoff. The pen should be large enough to keep the dog from leaping out however low enough so that the operator can reach to pet the animal.

Unlike for their title, a puppy exercise pen isn't typically utilized to work out your puppy. There are quite a few different applications, but which are equally as significant. The majority of the time that these pens have been utilized to comprise bigger puppies, but in a few cases they are sometimes utilized for bigger dogs. A puppy exercise pen should be taller than your puppy when they're standing on their back feet, and your puppy shouldn't have the ability to jump from the pencil.

One Of these applications is containment. Use them to help keep your pet secure when you can not keep tabs on these. That is great if you want to head to work and do not need to leave your puppy (s) unsupervised and do not wish to crate them yet will need to maintain them contained to a smaller place. These work nicely in the event that you don't have the capability to include them on your kitchen space, for instance. It permits the puppy to be secure; however, have more space to roam than at a crate. Or perhaps you've got a puppy which you're babysitting for a couple of days, and you do not wish to allow your dogs socialize with another dog whenever you're not home to manage, and you also do not wish to crate the dog. Furthermore, in case you've got a litter of dogs that require some enjoyable time out in the lawn, you may use a puppy exercise pen and understand they won't ramble and runoff. The metallic drill pens may also be attached to a cage to provide the dogs more space. Exercise pens can also be used in pet shows to maintain the display dogs separate from one another.

Another Usage of exercise pencils would be to flaunt pets in adoption and rescue occasions. Many puppy rescue groups maintain adoption hours in local pet shops and attract dogs and dogs, which are offered for adoption. The vinyl snaps together "play yard" kind pens are best for this as they're simple to set up and takedown.

The third usage of a puppy exercises pens as though your puppy is recovering from an illness or injury and continues to be prescribed "cage remainder". The usage of this pencil is a temporary alternative to this crate. In case you've got active dogs just like I do, then you're going to learn just how difficult it's to make them remain on "cage break"!

You can also utilize an Exercise pen as temporary barriers or gates around doors, provided that Your puppy doesn't jump onto it or push it all on. Only unfold the panels and put it where it's necessary. Unless, of course, you've got a knuckle-headed Rottie mix similar to me, then that choice doesn't do the job.

LOCATING THE BEST DOG EXERCISE AREAS

Dog Exercise Areas are essential for any fantastic pet owner, whether in an overseas trip or throughout the country. These regions are an excellent spot for the dog to have some exercise and burn off some extra energy.

Finding brand new dog exercise areas could be, of course, a thing of a struggle when it comes to locating these areas while on holiday. But like with everything else in existence, it all boils down to understanding where to search for everything you require.

Based on where you are from, you can likely locate a web site which functions as an internet search engine for both dog parks along with other nearby regions on your state or nation. All you need to do is go into the town and say you're going to be seeing, and you are going to find all fitting consequences for the region. Locate a fantastic website, and it truly is that easy. Once you enter your research info, you're likely going to receive a multitude of useful details such as the addresses of local dog training areas, just how large they are, and what regulations have been included, and also how to locate them.

It's also helpful to search for the site of the neighborhood authorities in the region you're travelling . Some regional authorities have all kinds of pet-related info concerning the regional regions they serve, in addition to advice on their particular dog exercise areas and also the principles you're expected to follow along there.

Individuals that wish to locate dog training places to their pets and consider them along on holiday know that travel with their pets may be a hell of a great deal of fun. To begin with, pets are fantastic companions while vacationing, and you are never going to get lonely. Additionally, having pets on holiday is a fantastic motivation for one to venture out and revel in the sights as well as the moments of the regions where you're travelling. Pet dogs loathe remaining cooped up inside, which explains precisely why carrying them together for a vacation is a fantastic idea -- for both you and the pooch.

Before you choose your pet on the Street, It pays to do your homework to discover whether the areas you are going to likely to be genuinely pet-friendly. Your notion of what constitutes accommodation or services may be entirely different from your landlord round the corner or the cafe-owner farther down the road. Learn first.

In addition, you need to take your puppy into the vet and get him clearance to travelling, as a last-minute checkup from the vet can create a Massive gap for the upcoming travel programs. Other hints include packaging every one the provisions that your pet will need and making sure His ID tags are all updated with current details. Locating the Best dog-exercise places for you to conduct around in later doing all That is going to be a great deal more rewarding, also.

GETTING THE MOST OUT OF DOG EXERCISE AREAS

When taking your pet to the neighborhood dog training places, you need to remain prepared to spend some time with your pet doing exactly what she would like to perform. The main reason you visit this pets permitted place is so your pet can find some exercise and escape your home for a short time. Determine what type of actions your dog loves and be ready for a few interactive playtimes as you're out.

Your local dog exercise place is a good way for the dog to get some off-leash fun, thus be ready to participate and enjoy a while together. Dress appropriately for your puppy park. Make sure you wear loose-fitting, comfortable shoes and clothes you can run in and do not mind getting dirty. A business suit is an unsuitable clothing option for a pets-allowed location. You need always to wear something which you don't mind getting dirty. Your dog might be trained not to jump on individuals with muddy paws, but it does not mean that each dog there'll reveal to you the exact same courtesy.

The pets permitted regions are for Those Who Wish to invest Time with their dogs. Simply since these regions are for off-leash enjoyable, your pet should not be left unattended for any quantity of time. You always need to have them view. For active dogs who prefer to run across, you'll have to maintain a close watch on these, regardless of what they're doing in this time or where they could go. Always attempt to remain close to your own dog to intervene if a fight breaks out. Invite your puppy to learn more about the region and play the supplied equipment. This may mean getting from the sand yourself to promote your puppy. Don't sit in 1 corner and be exhausted while your pet attempts for one to perform with him.

Dog exercise areas will be the perfect place for one to get some exercise too. But always see That your pet is Entertained as you are performing your exercises. You would not need your Puppy to invite herself to somebody else's picnic as you're performing pushups. Look at visiting those pets allowed regions to perform exercise that Is intended to be interactive with your pet. You can play with Bring with him or her you can merely delight in a run around the region together. Be sure to leave your toys in your home, and rather use the apparatus Provided in the dog training places to socialize with your puppy.

When taking your pet with you for dog training places, you could realize your pet has a great deal of pleasure but is not getting the exercise he or she really needs. The combo of fresh scents may be deflecting , but your puppy begins drifting from tree to blossom post, stopping anywhere in between to incorporate his own message into the assortment of aromas he's faced with. Preventing your dog from getting diverted may be a true challenge, but with just a little effort and encouragement on your character, it may be overcome.

Have accepted your dog to the dog park to provide him with a chance to work out. You need him to play and run with, to burn off a while until he could invest it into chewing gumshoes or munching in your own sofa. To be able to get the absolute most from pet parks, you want to ensure your puppy is really receiving the exercise you would like them to possess there. When he spends the entire excursion hurtling around a given area of the playground, you'll probably wind up with a puppy that's more lively and more than once you entered the playground at the very first location.

The secret is... If you'd like your dog to work out, you'll need to work out also. Rather than letting your puppy devote all his time or standing about, join in the fun by inviting your dog to play and run. Many dog exercise places do not allow external toys to be earned as a means of keeping struggles to a minimum. But getting your puppy to practice can be as straightforward as getting him running a couple of paces yourself. Do everything you can to maintain your furry friend energized and enthused about playing both you and the other puppies in the region. In the event the distractions on your dog exercise region continue to end up being overly appealing, look at moving your puppy to another part of the playground. Put a leash for your pet if you want to take him off. Proceed to a place with fewer barriers and encourage drama within this place instead. Keep in it, and you'll gradually get your pet to run away some of the surplus energy at the playground.

If you can't get your puppy to participate in drama, look at carrying her to make friends with other puppies that Are enjoying. Occasionally, with other dogs engaged in drama can Be the final boost your four-legged friend desires to be able to Realise that this is somewhere to operate, not to sniff. Having a little Encouragement, these suggestions are going to have your puppy ready to return home to get a Long rest in virtually no time in any way.

HEALTHY DOG EXERCISES

Here are some fantastic dog exercise suggestions which can help keep both owner and dog healthy and fit and in great form.

Cycling

Walking along with your bike, particularly trotting, wherever your puppy transfers its left hind leg and front leg (and vice versa) in precisely the exact same time, is perfect physical exercise. The motions are in a direct line along with your dog becomes optimum usage of its own muscles, which boosts muscular improvement. This is often performed in certain areas of the planet, but in certain regions, it's not allowed in the event the puppy is still on the leash because this would limit your hands off the bicycle.

Where It's possible to allow the dog to run off the leash supporting the bike, and it ought to not be an issue. It's frequently stated that a dog shouldn't walk with a bike until its first birthday, however that is only partially correct. Should you just cycle for small distances and adjust the pace to that of their dog, it is possible to start with this if the puppy is six weeks old.

Always adjust your rate to match the dog and block it from getting tired. Gradually develop the cycle excursions and, together with this, the state of your puppy. An athlete wouldn't be able to run a marathon right after the winter without getting hurt, and the exact same is applicable to the dog.

For reasons of security, educate your dog from the start it has to always run onto the control side of the bike. It goes without mentioning , before you begin to bicycle with your own dog, it has to be properly socialized and flawlessly beneath (voice) controller. When it suddenly overlooks a different dog or jumps to a side since it's scared by something, both you and the puppy is going to be compromised, in addition to other street users.

Many bike trips are on asphalt streets. Bear in mind that asphalt may become really hot in the summertime, very damaging your pet's pads, and it'll have quite a while for this kind of injury to cure. Along with this, a puppy has the propensity to proceed, even if it actually can't. The combo of more exertion and heat isn't great for any pet; however, for Huskies plus a few Mastiffs can lead to severe and dangerous problems. Consequently, cycle just in moderate temperatures, and just in the evenings and weekends in the peak of this summer.

Swimming

On hot summertime, swimming is a perfect exercise. The dog utilizes all of its muscles and isn't very likely to injure itself from the water. Most dogs love water from character and can barely pass along with a pool or pond without needing a dip. Other puppies require a little more reinforcement.

You can Teach your pet to float by entering the water to it and encouraging it below the breast and stomach as it does not have any contact with the floor. If your pet loves to recover, it is possible to throw a silenced block to the water, then throwing it a little further each moment, so it gradually acclimatizes. Never only push the dog to the water. This Spartan method just promotes anxiety about water and may also cause your puppy to have significantly less confidence on your own.

Water that's dangerous for people due to harmful germs, or since there are inconsistent undercurrents, can be dangerous for puppies. Just allow your puppy to swim in safe areas. Additionally, it can become entangled in fishing nets and monitoring water Crops, so be cautious with your furry friend in these regions. Ultimately, make sure that It can escape the water without a lot of trouble steeply Sloping banks may not be possible to scale for several dogs.

DOG EXERCISE FOR YOUR DOG'S HIP AND JOINTS

Dogs are obviously busy, and they need to manoeuvre around. However, because your lifestyle gets fuller, your pet's allegedly active lifestyle becomes influenced. When dogs don't get the practice they desire, they can develop behaviour and physical difficulties, like joint and hip ailments. Since they are like children, they'd find something to do on their own, and you may not enjoy these items. They may take part in destructive digging and chewing and play biting. Moreover, simply because you've got a huge yard doesn't automatically signify your puppy is becoming exercise. If you only leave them in the lawn, they won't do anything more than wait for one to play together, wait for one to allow them back indoors.

As much as a workout is essential, make sure they are acceptable for the dog. Young puppies, specific breeds, or even those experiencing hip and joint conditions like hip dysplasia and arthritis might not sustain protracted exercise. Below are a few dog exercise suggestions that are secure and will help boost the wellness of your pet's joints and hip.

Leash walking for more than half an hour Is a secure and healthful form of exercise for the dog. This is particularly valuable for young dogs whose bones haven't yet completely grown and for people who have hip dysplasia and arthritis. They get the workout they want without placing too much strain in their joints.

Another fantastic type of exercise is swimming since it also doesn't overstress your pet's joints. There are a couple of things that you need to take under account when you choose your puppy to swim, however. To begin with, ensure their very first encounter with water is fine. Additionally, unless you're certain of the swimming skills, don't let them get in warm water above their head. Other kinds of exercise which are safe for the pet's joints and hip include things like playing fetch and allow them to monitor snacks you conceal around your residence.

Additionally, there are still other ways to keep your pet's hips and tendons the pure manner. These include weight management and providing them with organic joint and hip supplements.

CANINE TREADMILL

The first treadmills were created for smaller animals like sheep and dogs at the mid-19th century to churn butter and also for bigger livestock such as horses such as grain threshing. The idea of treadmills for punishment has been especially for people and appearing around the 1950s at prisons. There's not any background I could find anyplace of treadmills being made for use in abusing creatures. That is not to say it has never been achieved; people can discover lots of unusual and creative ways to become cruel to the most loving critters. But that could be on account of an individual human's activities, not on account of the design or intention of this machine. It is well worth pointing out walking a puppy for the mandatory 30-60 minutes of daily workout at 90-degree warmth and humidity on your own pavement can be regarded as misuse instead of allowing your puppy to use a puppy treadmill in a comfortable and safe environment.

The blogosphere is rife with announcements opinion, this to possess and use a puppy treadmill is both irresponsible and thoughtful and comparable to allowing tv to raise a young child. Should this happen, this is simply because a person decides to do this whatever the aim of this treadmill's layout. Far from becoming the "idle option," choosing to supply a dog treadmill to your very best buddy's exercise is frequently the most responsible option. Canine treadmills are made to supply dogs a means to work out in many different circumstances. There's not any question that the perfect pet workout will be 30-60 minutes, depending upon the pet's breed, age and general wellbeing, running in new air. It's projected that dogs may pay up to 3 times the place away from the leash they could on a leash, but many pet owners do not have the capability to provide their very best friends with that type of liberty. The environment represents a few of the greatest limitations for this permitting our puppies a complimentary romp, because of visitors, other metropolitan congestion and pet laws. Weather is another substantial element. Responsible pet owners are conscious of the circumstances if it is too hot or too cold to their puppies to safely endure exertion, or even to threat paw harm. This is among the kinds of ailments the treadmill was intended for: Just as a nutritional supplement to your own dog's outside exercise if circumstances aren't safe.

Another, Also it may be contended the main, condition for that dog walkers have been developed for use is as a different way of exercise if conventional, demanding outdoor romps aren't possible. When a puppy is rehabbing from surgery, the dog treadmill provides an extremely controlled and tracked exercise atmosphere. If a puppy owner is sick, handicapped or older, a dog wheelchair ensures that the dog still has his necessary exercise. Shelters and animal hospitals utilize treadmills to be certain puppies get exercise if the volunteers or staff can not get the dogs out for long runs or walks.

If you are doing research on puppy Treadmills prior to buying one, I congratulate you. Whether you decide it is ideal for you and your puppy, or maybe not, just make certain you're reading balanced facts rather than opinion. Your vet will be among Your best resources. The Truth Is that while veterinarians concur That being outdoors with your puppy to get demanding exercise is perfect, most Admit it isn't necessarily practical or even feasible to be in a position to perform that. A puppy treadmill is most often the most accountable alternative for Keeping the health and well-being of your furry friend.

CHAPTER SEVEN:
DOG TRAINING TECHNIQUES

A QUICK OVERVIEW

Many People today adore the notion of having a puppy but something which they must bear in mind often instances, is the puppy has to be trained. While the puppy might seem heart-breakingly adorable when it is at a shelter or in the pound, choosing the puppy is simply the first region of the association between a puppy owner and the creature. A lot of don't know they need to put effort and time into interacting with your dog.

An unsocialized puppy will confound other people, split the house, and will make an environment which may turn out to be so poor that it might need to be returned. Many times, when puppies need to get returned to additional sources, it is going to wind up euthanized, which is quite heartbreaking. All this may be spared if an individual learns the numerous techniques to be able to socialize your dog.

One thing they have to know is that he must be informed exactly what to do. It is from the puppy character to stick to a leader. The dog will probably be more than prepared to comply with the direction of its grasp. Here's a look at some common methods which are used in puppy training:

"Dog Whispering"

That is a Technique that's existed for a little while, however, gained national notoriety throughout the previous ten decades. A few individuals could hear this expression and wonder just how on earth whispering into a puppy can instruct it! Whispering is not supposed to be taken in this circumstance. As coaches have demonstrated, whispering is a phrase that describes linking with a being or a thing on a really profound and almost spiritual degree. If it comes to dog training methods, dog daycare entails careful monitoring of their dog's behaviour and activities.

It literally involves getting inside the brain and the behaviour system of the puppy. When someone utilizes dog whispering methods, they socialize with the puppy on the puppy level. Again, one of the most frequent errors that people make is handling your puppy, just like a tiny human being.

"Reward training."

Reward training Is very straightforward, and it is among the old tricks that function. This is an easy way of educating the puppy by positive reinforcement. After he does exactly what it's told to perform, it receives a cure. These works are that the puppy owner has to lure the dog to the deal with. When the puppy develops consciousness of the cure, it develops a powerful appetite for this. After the need for it's very powerful, the puppy owner attracts back. Then the puppy receives control, and once the dog obeys the control, and it receives the deal. The thing is to earn the dog partner a deal with the control.

"Clicker Training"

Other puppy training Techniques include one that's much like reward coaching, which can be known as clicker training. These works are that the clicker is integrated to find your dog's interest. The clicker is interpreted because of a kind of communicating with the puppy. It learns there is a control or reward connected in combination with this clicker. A lot of men and women assert this is enjoyable, and they really make a match with the puppy using the clicker to their puppy training jobs.

"Ultrasonic Whistle"

Last, A rather new sort of dog training procedure is known as the ultrasonic whistle. This works since the ultrasonic noise is only heard by the puppy. After the owner is hoping to convey a control or halt the dog from barking, then they'll discount their whistle whenever they wish to convey a command into the puppy. The good thing about this is that people can not hear this sound. However, the dog can listen to this, and they'll learn how to connect the noise with control.

Dog Training techniques are not difficult to integrate, but they're something that Certainly must be integrated from the time that the puppy owner attracts their Brand new pet house. No matter how old or young the puppy is, they'll need training. Once they are trained correctly, They'll Be a wonderful Addition to a person's family.

DOG WHISPERING TRAINING

Dog Whispering is getting a remarkably common dog training program. Actually, in a certain manner, dog whispering and clicker training are carrying the puppy world by storm. However, even though the prevalence of this specific method is quite new, the methods themselves have been around for centuries.

Rather than being a particular training method which utilizes specific methods, dog whispering relies on an understanding of dog psychology, canine body language and behaviour patterns. It requires your pet's natural behaviour into consideration and essentially disregards conventional learning concepts. Because of this, this is even more of a general "doctrine" about dog training compared to anything else. As soon as you know his instincts, the way your puppy "believes," and exactly what his body language signifies, you are going to be able to "speak" to a puppy through your body language and activities - a speech he will understand intuitively. This technique also highlights the ability of positive reinforcement. This mixture - efficient communication combined with producing positive relationships with the behaviours you need - makes puppy whispering techniques tremendously powerful.

The significance of placing yourself as the boss - someone who's reliable, confident and competent - is the basic foundation of this technique. All puppies are pack animals by nature, therefore establishing your location along with the dog's pack leader (the dominant "alpha dog") is vital once you're employing this particular technique. Getting the pet is typically an issue of producing your puppy feel safe and protected in a variety of scenarios, so he knows you're his package leader and will shield him from a possible threat. Of course, you will also have to set up your dominance, which means that your instructions can't be dismissed.

An excellent pack leader (or alpha) exercises company but calm advice, so pet whispering integrates a blend of affection, positive reinforcement and company, non-violent adjustments. If done properly, this may provide you with a puppy that is obedient and joyful to be like that.

As with any additional coaching procedure, dog daycare needs you to be patient, have a calm demeanour and also keep your own self-control. In addition, you ought to consider that your puppy will call for a good deal of repetitions and a good deal of positive reinforcement until he sees the behaviour you are trying to educate. Shouting, bodily punishment or losing the mood doesn't have any place in puppy whispering (or some other kind of puppy training, for that matter). In reality, rather than increasing your voice or even talking aloud for your puppy, a great deal of the communication you will do while you are using dog whispering techniques are going to be through nonverbal body language along with a few occasional hand signs.

The main manner dogs attempt to communicate with individuals (along with other dogs) entails particular moves and body language. That is the reason why this technique needs you to possess at least a fundamental comprehension of pet psychology and puppy behaviour. With this knowledge, it might be simple to misinterpret or perhaps completely overlook what our puppies are attempting to inform us. When that comes to pass, dogs have a tendency to attempt more extreme procedures to convey, such as barking when they are feeling stressed or threatened.

Unless you are meeting a new dog, eye contact is one of the very best ways you need to communicate with puppies. Eye contact helps all you translate another's facial expressions. Provide your pet with a few bodily or verbal cues even though you're keeping eye contact, nevertheless. With no other cues, a puppy may translate being stared at right as threatening or confrontational behaviour on the part. This is particularly possible once the dog does not know you.

Regardless of the significance of understanding dog behaviour and Psychology, you will need to stay "individual" when you are employing dog whispering methods. To put it differently, dog whispering does not ask that you crawl on all fours, play bow, or even wag your own "tail" to communicate your message to a furry friend. Dogs are smart, receptive creatures and they recognize you are not a puppy. They are also smart enough to understand individual body language. So, there is no need to attempt to "be a puppy" when you are employing dog whispering methods.

Rather, treat your pet with respect and dignity. Do not attempt to become a control freak, but do not treat your pet just like a kid . Offer your puppy just as much affection as you need, but in addition, you should give him advise in business, calm, controlled, and respectful manner. Any bodily interventions - like altering your pet's standing by lifting one of the teammates to instruct him to "shake hands," for example - must be carried out in a fashion that's tender, non-violent and non-threatening.

Dog whispering techniques may be accustomed to successfully teach your puppy all of the frequent obedience commands, such as "sit," "stay," "come," and "down."

This training procedure can also be employed to deter unwanted behaviours like excessive barking. A lot of men and women use devices such as anti-bark collars to prevent their pet's improper barking. Other folks yell or perhaps attack their puppies. Neither procedure is very powerful. Anti-bark collars do not tackle the main reason behind the barking, also yelling just leaves the barking worse since the pet believes his proprietor is barking . With these methods, in the event, your dog stops barking, it is usually from fear as opposed to a feeling of respect and obedience.

Dog whispering tactics to prevent barking include trying to find the reason that your pet is barking at the first location. If you do not detect any danger from the direction that your puppy's barking at, flip off and take to a relaxed, serene posture. The body language will inform your puppy you do not find any threat - and consequently no motive for him .

Dog whispering likely will not work for every dog owner. It takes you to be quietly confident and emotionally and emotionally dominant over your pet. Homeowners who lack confidence are not assertive are unlikely to succeed with puppy whispering techniques.

Additionally, this coaching doctrine is very likely to take more than conventional dog training methods. After all, you will Have to spend some time with your puppy before you are in a position to comprehend each other.

DOG REWARD TRAINING

Reward Training (that is sometimes called lure coaching) is a really effective training method for educating dogs a range of desirable behaviours. And, along with being exceptionally effective, reward coaching is a simple, enjoyable method to utilize. This specific training technique offers much faster, more reliable results than techniques that rely greatly on scolding, punishment, or corrections, and it's doing it in a means that is considerably more favourable to both you and your pet.

Since reward training is so powerful, it is currently among the hottest dog training methods. In its centre, reward coaching functions since you reward your pet with a cure or tidbit of meals if he does exactly what you ask. Most owners follow the food benefit with verbal praise. The compliments and food are positive reinforcement that helps your pet learn how to connect the actions he played with great things (praise and food) and motivates him to replicate that behaviour.

Along with becoming successful, reward coaching provides a more positive training setting than other training methods. As it is a reward-based procedure, you benefit your dog every time he can, as you request. Scolding, striking, penalizing or adjusting your pet for not after your control is not utilized in reward coaching. You merely benefit and reinforce the activities you do need your puppy to carry out. This positive reinforcement creates reward coaching a far more enjoyable experience for dogs and owners than penalizing him.

You need to be cautious to simply give your pet treats in the ideal time during coaching sessions, yet. In case the time of these rewards is irrelevant to a dog doing because you ask, he will get confused about what you would like, and that he may even begin believing he will get treats regardless of what. Thus, ensure just to reward your dog for doing something right.

In certain ways, reward coaching Is the reverse of aversive puppy training, in which dogs have been trained to connect undesirable behaviours with negative reinforcement like scolding, corrections or punishment. The negative reinforcement ceases if your dog performs the desired behaviour. In concept, this procedure prevents dogs from replicating unwanted activities and trains them to perform exactly what owners need, but at the very long term, it is an unpleasant procedure and not anywhere near as successful as reward training. Rather than punishing your dog to whatever he's wrong, reward coaching allows you to show your dog what you want him to perform then reward him if he does it.

Require housetraining, for instance. The 2 approaches approach the job in a variety of ways. There are a large number of places that a dog can relieve himself within the home, and they are all unsuitable. In case you employed aversive training methods, you would want to await your pet to remove someplace in the home and correct him when he's doing. Consider this for a moment. Is it not unfair to penalize your puppy before he has had an opportunity to understand your principles? Plus, you have to see that applying this technique for housetraining can call for a lot of corrections and also a great deal of time. Is it not faster, easier, and much more effective to just show your puppy the ideal spot to relieve himself and reward him if he uses it?

There is another reason why benefit coaching Produces better outcomes compared to aversive training. Consistency is vital once you're training a puppy. If you are using punishment and corrections to discourage undesirable behaviour, you will always have to punish your dog every time he plays that behaviour. Well, we are not robots, and it is not possible to be prepared to perform this each second of this day. You would never leave the house rather than take your eyes away from your puppy before you would even have a prospect of penalizing him each time he leaves a behavioural error. Create 1 slip-up and don't punish your puppy for an error, and he will find out that he will eliminate all the misbehaviour. That is likely not the lesson that you need him to understand.

Contrary to aversive training, reward coaching does not need you to be infallibly constant on your responses to a pet's misbehaviours. You do not have to reward your puppy each time that he does because you ask - in reality, he will learn just as fast (or even more so) when the rewards he receives for desirable behaviour are unpredictable and irregular rather than being awarded each time he plays the behaviour. And, most importantly, should you make mistakes using aversive instruction you risk losing your pet's trust. That will not happen with reward coaching, where errors may temporarily confound your puppy, but they will not induce him to turn into competitive or anxiety or mistrust you.

Besides housetraining your puppy, you can utilize reward training to instruct him a range of jobless controls ("sit," remain," come" and "down," for example) along with a range of entertaining tips. However, you might also discourage problem behaviours with reward coaching. By way of instance, if you would like to train your puppy not to instruct him exactly what he is permitted to chew off (a toy, by way of instance), then reward him if he chews on it. Or, if you would like your dog to stop jumping up in your guests once they come from the doorway, instruct him to sit once people arrive and then reward him for this behaviour.

Though some owners do not enjoy reward training since they believe dogs trained this way to follow their orders just because they need a treat rather than outside Of awareness of respect or dependence, there is no wonder that reward Training is successful. And, even in the event that you accept the assumption that dogs learn from reward coaching strictly since they are being "bribed," Is not better than obeying from a fear of punishment? Not only this, but treats are not the only sort of reward which may be utilized as Positive reinforcement. Praising your puppy with an enthusiastic, joyful tone of Voice, offering him toys, and giving him plenty of affection can All be equally as inspiring as providing him food or snacks.

DOG CLICKER TRAINING

Dog Clicker training is just one of the greatest dog training techniques should you want to educate your puppy or pet the typical commands like sit and stay. This type of training requires a little bit of patience in the beginning but will bring about fantastic results because you see your puppy training efforts pay off.

The famous scientist Pavlov, he soon began training them using the bell intentionally. With pet clicker training, you're training your puppy to obey a specific control together with the noise of a unique dog training clicker. The sound of the instrument could be heard from a long distance off as well as over the noise of visitors and other noisy distractions.

To begin using clicker training, Whatever you need is an inexpensive clicker and a purse of your pet's favorite treats. Bear in mind that the click will be your reward to your dog minding the control that you give, together with a cure to fortify his desire to become obedient.

Do not Click without it being evident that the puppy has obeyed your control and has been rewarded. Click and offer them a cure. Try to be more consistent with all the words that you use for the orders you provide, so you don't confuse the puppy.

The Way to Begin With Dog Clicker Training

Consistently Be cautious about what you really want the puppy to perform, sit, stay ahead. Give the order securely. Should they get it done, click and provide a reward. Repeat this a few times so as to strengthen the command along with click.

They Will begin to connect the sound of the click together with all the action you want them to carry out. Another advantage of dog clicker training is the way the instant it is. The clicker receives their attention straight away, which makes them awake and excited to get a treat. The click is much quicker than the term "Sit."

Continue with the practice before the dog reacts as Quickly as possible for your control. Also, be certain that you don't underestimate the treats.

Command-Based Dog Training

Once your puppy is well-trained with the clicker, the upcoming stages would be to convince him to react to a spoken command so you may continue your puppy training even with no clicker. The puppy will begin to expect the control even before you click on. He'll also be excited about his benefit. Control, click, treat, or praise will become second nature for you, and the puppy will connect his obedience having a joyful owner and a great reward or treat.

ULTRASONIC WHISTLE TRAINING

Ultrasonic Whistle training is a method utilized by many starts in addition to professional dog trainers, especially for training a puppy to search. It employs a particular whistle known as an ultrasonic whistle or puppy whistle to have a puppy's attention and provide orders. Some call the unit a quiet whistle since it generates sounds in rather large frequency ranges which for the large part, are inaudible for individuals. Dogs, but have very acute hearing and may realize the whistle's noises when they are a significant distance from their handler.

When you blow to an ultrasonic whistle that your puppy will notice a different, loud whistle, though you'll likely only notice that your breath is hurrying through it. Whistle training involves teaching your puppy to reply to the noise made by the whistle. When he accomplishes this, you are going to have the ability to get your pet's attention or call your puppy without crying, even when he is from sight or away.

The noise made by an ultrasonic whistle is High-pitched; however, when used correctly, it will not damage your pet's ears impair his hearing at all. For a lot of men and women, whistle training only gives them a method of receiving their pet's focus, but its long-lived capacities can ensure it is a very valuable supplement to additional coaching methods.

Whistle coaching can be highly successful, especially For instruction gun dogs and older dogs which operate in the distance away from their owners. It may be somewhat tricky to get the hang of Praise training once you are just starting, but a few clinics are able to help you get it correctly. As soon as you do, then it is going to get value for long-distance instruction. In reality, when coupled with hand signs, whistle training will be able to help you train your puppy to carry out several commands in the distance, such as "sit" come" and "proceed in a particular direction."

Listed below are a couple of tips you can use to get started with training:

Use Compliments and snacks to inspire your dog. After blowing the whistle and then instantly praising and giving a puppy a treat several times, he will connect the noise of the deal with getting the benefit.

Your puppy learns that the whistle means great things are coming back, walk a couple of steps off and blow the whistle. If he does not come to you instantly, phone him with an inviting voice. Give him a cure along with hot praise the moment he can come. Repeat this a few times (it may take a day or two for the dog to find down this).

Play a game of "hide and Hunt" with your puppy. The hideout of your puppy later telling him to "sit" and "stay" Then call him immediately blow the whistle, ongoing to create the noise until your puppy successfully finds you. Give him a treat and praise the moment he or she does. Yet more, practice by playing the match many times.

By following these tips, you may use whistle Training to instruct your puppy to come for you, even when you're from his Sight or away. If your puppy appears confused at any moment throughout the Training procedure, do not become frustrated or get started scolding your puppy. Instead, return to some measure your puppy has mastered and then build from that point. Bear in mind, and practice makes perfect.

CHAPTER EIGHT:
DOG MANAGEMENT

DOG TOYS

Dogs Easily become bored when they're stuck indoors by chilly weather and with no suitable pet toys and toy stimulation, so they could easily become harmful. With fast winter approaching, chances are you already be dreading the long, cold days stuck at home along with your cherished pets. The fantastic thing is there are lots of tools available to help keep your pet amused, happy and most of all, prevent them from ruining your house and possessions.

First, You Have to Comprehend why a puppy's Behaviour can come to be so harmful. The issue really places with us people. Originally dogs had been born and lived in the wild in which they were obviously busy and maintained busy searching for food and shielding themselves. Regrettably, if we pumped them, their lifestyles slowly became sedentary since they were introduced into our houses and fed from bowls rather than searching for their meals.

To compensate for Their deficiency of pure actions, it's vital to give lots of puppy toys and toys to keep them amused and properly aroused. There are a number of dog toy options available today, and a number of the more recent puzzle toys are simply the stimulation that your dog should stay busy and out of trouble.

Unfortunately, in the Event That You do not provide your puppy with toys to Both fulfil their day with all constructive pursuits and fulfil their desire to feel, they will probably find your favorite pair of sneakers and make their very own toy! This contributes to the following question of how you can provide your pet with proper puppy toys to match their demands.

First, ensure you've got a fantastic range of toys for them to appreciate. They'll get bored using the exact same one or 2 toys daily so just give them one or two days and rotate out the toys to keep those interested. Be certain you choose quality toys for the dog to prevent unnecessary choking dangers and also to make sure they are long-lasting.

Many People today give their puppies old socks along with other family items to play . That is a frequent mistake, which just disrupts your pet and also causes you grief afterwards. As an instance, if you provide them with a classic sock or perhaps an older t-shirt to chew , they will obviously feel that each sock that they locate in your residence is fair game to perform . It's also advisable to ensure that your puppy has a particular place to maintain their pet toys. Use a jar or plastic bathtub they have easy accessibility to and this will assist your puppy to comprehend that toys belong to them.

With a lot of dog toys to select from, what are a few of the stimulating and boredom buster toys out there?

* Balls - I've yet to observe a puppy who doesn't adore their ball, and it's an excellent way that you socialize and play with your puppy also. Ensure you've got separate inside and out balls, so they don't drag a filthy ball to the home.

* Chew Toy - Dog's desire to snore automatically so be certain that you supply them with great quality chew toys which don't have small parts which may come away or toys which are filled with noisemakers. The brand new stuffing totally free toys are a superb selection for chewing gum and using a match of tug-o-war. Additionally, I urge a toy which emotionally challenges your puppy. You will find a lot of new puppy toy puzzles accessible where your pet gets one particular toy that's full of toys that are smaller also must determine how to put them there. Another popular would be the rubber toys which hold either snacks or food inside and your dog must work to get out the food. Everyone these offer exceptional stimulation and also rests for you.

* Chew Bones - Provide both an action and a means for you and your furry friend to unwind. With numerous variants of bones, rawhide bones, rubber bones, mouth bones and lots of more, you're certain to find one which is the dog's favorite. Make certain to choose a bone that fulfils your pet's size and gum skills to prevent choking events. If your puppy doesn't complete the

bone throughout their chewing session, then pick this up and place it away for one more day.

* Comfort Toy - Comfort toys grow every time a puppy is young and coping with separation anxiety in their mom to a different residence, but many puppies don't outgrow their relaxation toys. But this kind of toy offers advantages to an adult dog. In case you need to travel to unknown areas, make them with a bitter vet or veterinarian for a couple of days, they provide your pet with a sense of relaxation and also have a reassuring result. Many dogs like to utilize their comfort toy to get a match of tug-o-war or to mimic vibration their prey when from the wild.

By providing multiple puppy Toys for your pet, you'll almost certainly avoid creating bad Customs and stop them from participating in harmful behaviour. Most Moreover, your pet is going to be a joyful, healthful dog, however chilly it gets.

DOG BATH

Can you totally hate the notion of giving your pet a bath? It's such a cluttered and usually very disagreeable Job

Admit it, would you kind of let your pet go with a tub till it becomes unbearable and you need to wash him.

Welcome to our planet. That's the way many dog owners consider giving our dogs a bathroom. You don't ever mention the term tub since then your puppy will run and hide.

It normally requires more than 1 person along with a great deal of work for this particular ordeal to occur.

The Size of this dog may also be a nuisance. A massive dog is certainly not simple to wash. If your puppy has a thick coating, it's challenging to wash out the fur to the epidermis.

A lot of folks don't have lawns and water hookups out there.

But, After the time comes and your puppy begins smelling like a puppy, it needs to be accomplished. For the dog's sake, in addition to yours, a tub is essential.

Some Individuals have the luxury of getting their dog vaccinated by specialists, but that may be costly and outside or reach many men and women.

In case you are like most people and need to this task yourself here are some simple hints to make it simpler

1. Begin frequently bathing your puppy from a young age, or the moment you adopt you. This way they'll make use to the total procedure. Never provide a pup at tub till they are 8 months , and only if needed.

2. Always ensure your house is warm before beginning an indoor tub. If desired, turn up your thermostat a few levels. Get all of your prep work; this consists of shampoo and everything you want to start the bathroom.

3. Combing and cleaning out all of the mats. Do this until Your pet becomes wet, to protect against the mats by turning to strong clumps which may only be eliminated with clippers.

If your puppy has gotten into some kind of tacky materials such as paint or pitch, cut the affected region of the hair or soak it using mineral or vegetable oil for 24 hours. When it's a massive region, you may be better off consulting with a professional groomer.

4. Preparing the individual (puppy). To maintain Their eyes protected from suds set a little drop of mineral oil inside them. You might even put cotton balls in their ears. When utilizing cotton balls, be certain of these dimensions if they're too little for the dog's ears that they can slide down the ear canal.

5. Bathe your pet as fast as possible. This will relieve the strain on the two of you.

Do an intensive and decent cleansing, be it outside or inside particularly rinsing all of the shampoos away.

Soap Residue may lead to itching and irritation for your own skin. Always dry off your dog instantly. You are employing a furry friend shammy and soft towels if your puppy doesn't obey a hairdryer on low setting functions quite nicely.

Be Ready for the significant shake your dog is going to do. It's very good to allow them to shake off the water, just be ready and keep them at a little area like the toilet to restrain the water moving around.

Your pet will be much happier when he/she's fresh and clean smelling, obviously, perform Not expect them to allow you to know they enjoyed it. Together with the right Preparation bathing, your pet doesn't need to become a struggle. It may be nearly enjoyable when done together with love, patience and kindness.

How to train a puppy

Professional approach to handling and training your dog to be perfectly disciplined.

By Jennifer Dogget

INTRODUCTION

You'll be training your pup from the minute that you take it home and begin to house train. Puppies begin learning from birth, and superior breeders start handling and socialization straight away. Some training may start after the pup can open its eyes and walk. Young puppies have short attention spans. However, you may expect them to start to understand easy obedience commands like "sit," down," and "stay," as young as seven to eight weeks old.

Proper dog instruction has traditionally been postponed until 6 weeks old. In fact, this stage is a really bad time to get started. The puppy is learning from each experience, and delaying training means missed opportunities for your dog to understand how you'd want him to act. Throughout the juvenile phase, the puppy is starting to solidify grownup behavioral patterns and advances through dread intervals. Behaviors discovered in puppyhood might have to get changed. Additionally, anything which has been trained or learned wrongly will have to get reversed and re-taught. Dogs are capable of learning beyond a young age.

When instruction is launched at seven to eight weeks old, use techniques which rely on positive reinforcement and teaching. Puppies have short attention spans, so instruction sessions must be short but should happen every day. Puppies can be instructed to "sit" "down" and "track" with a technique known as food-lure training. We work with food treats to lure your dog to accompany its nose to the appropriate places for "sit," down," stand," and "stay."

CHAPTER ONE:

WHAT YOU SHOULD KNOW BEFORE GETTING A DOG

When adding a puppy to your household, whether or not you adopt from a local shelter or buy from a private breeder, there are lots of critical things to remember. The essential element in choosing to adopt a puppy is ensuring the whole family is in agreement and willing to pitch in to help provide love and attention. Without this dedication, the puppy will lack the well-rounded family structure it needs.

For first-time pet owners, it's extremely important that you do comprehensive research to learn which sort of maintenance is going to be necessary, the fiscal responsibilities involved along with the ideal breed for the household. Some kids are uncomfortable with dogs, so in the event that you have kids, do ask them to help choose the puppy. Do not adopt a puppy if your kids are terrified of dogs and don't adopt a dog if he's afraid of children.

Another significant thing to consider is training. All dogs, no matter if big or small, need to get some kind of obedience training. That is essential not just for the safety and enjoyment of your pet, but also for the safety and enjoyment of those connected with your pet. Obedience training is going to teach you how you can control your pet and give him safe limitations. It is also going to instruct your puppy to grow up into a "good citizen". The AKC (American Kennerl Club) site offers you resources and information on obedience training.

You will also wish to enquire about veterinary assistance before adopting a puppy. Referrals from friends are fantastic resources. Do not be afraid to stop by your potential vet's office before becoming a customer. Take note of the cleanliness of the reception, the size of their staff, the hours of surgery along with the fees and payment options. If possible, ask to talk with the vet briefly and ask any questions that you might have about having a dog.

Dogs are called "man's best friend". They're faithful, lovely, and affectionate; they also guard the home and are excellent companions. If you're trying to find a buddy, keep in mind that young dogs aren't just the most economical but also the most receptive to instructions. Before you start looking at available puppies, below are a few questions to consider before choosing.

A puppy will become a faithful and enjoyable companion; however, you ought to be ready to take complete responsibility for their wellness and wellbeing. In case you haven't had a puppy before, then it is difficult to know about all of the factors you want to think about.

First of all, the dimensions of your garden and home will dictate the dimensions of your favorite pet. It goes without saying that a tiny apartment with no garden isn't a sensible alternative for a large dog.

The levels of energy of your favorite pet are also significant, and you ought to think of what size of puppy you're able to take care of. Age is another vital variable you should think about if you like a pup, as choosing an older dog can help narrow down your search a little.

Puppies need training, so be sure you have enough time to devote to this. Even though a younger puppy could be less difficult to train, you'll discover that many dogs of all ages are extremely flexible. In reality, older dogs have a tendency to be more healthy and need significantly less exercise, which may be more appropriate for many people's lives.

In regards to temperament, think about your house and way of living; should you have a lot of regular visitors, then it would be better to get a more social dog who will not mind having people over.

In case you have children in the house or visiting your house, then you have to be extra careful. Some dogs might be afraid of toddlers, and some dogs may have different tolerance levels to kids so, in case you've got loud, unruly children, you'll need a puppy that can put up with them.

If you already own a puppy and are searching for another, then make sure all your pets are going to be able to live in harmony.

Try and choose a pet that has the same disposition and needs as the one you already have.

As soon as you have worked out exactly what breed of puppy you would like, plan for the practical aspect of things and be ready for their birth. For instance, think about your typical daily schedule and consider when you could find time to take it for a stroll or to feed him.

Invest in good quality dog foods and keep your buddy in good health. Many people today prefer to get their pets equipped with microchips, so they're easier to find if they get lost. There are different types of dog identification, and you should ensure your dog could be recognized and returned home safe and sound in case it goes missing.

Grooming is another aspect that can help to maintain your pet in tiptop shape and may help save you money on vet care.

Obviously, there's much more to take into consideration if you're considering getting a puppy; however, it pays off to know the fundamentals before making your final choice.

Do I have enough time to get a puppy?

The dog will be part of your family and will need care on a regular basis. Your pet will require a good deal of care, especially in the very first months, since it might need to be educated and at this age they are more prone to ailments. You'll need to supply a nutritious diet, regular exercise, vet visits, and affection to the pet. Consider who will take care of your pet when you're away from home for a long period.

Could I afford a puppy?

Pets are costlier than people often believe. Think about the expenses of meals, training, health care, grooming, and dog sitting. Before getting housetrained, your pet can also cause a few expensive damages; scraped furniture and chewed-on shoes would definitely be the most common.

Which breed should I pick ?

Pick a dog that will suit your lifestyle and living quarters. The very worse thing to do is choose on the spur of the moment when coming across an adorable puppy. When choosing a breed, consider not just the dimensions but also the temperament. Terriers are modest in size, however they bark a good deal, are extremely busy, and require a good deal of exercise. Some bigger puppies, such as Labradors, are tender and are ideal with kids. Get to know well the different breeds before purchasing. Few pet owners do and they regret it later on.

When looking for dogs for sale, keep in mind that a dog is a massive responsibility concerning cash, time, and dedication. Carefully consider if you're able to look after your furry friend for 15 years or more. Before you select a puppy, pick which breed is the most acceptable for your loved ones. When looking for dogs available in your locality, look online. It's the quickest way to find pets available from private vendors, shelters , and pet breeders.

Deciding to adopt a puppy is a life decision and shouldn't be taken lightly. Be sure you and your family will have the ability to supply all of the dog's needs, such as love, companionship, and workout. Assessing and preparing yourself with this lifestyle modification will be critical to guarantee a happy and successful adoption.

THINK IT THROUGH BEFORE GETTING A DOG

People today get dogs for a number of reasons: companionship, protecting functions, searching, support intentions, and all around the world, people are getting to be pet owners for the very first time in their own lives. Humane shelters and adoption agencies are filled with abandoned puppies, but before you take the big step there are numerous things which you ought to think about.

Few things might tug at our hearts as much as the eyes of an abandoned dog or pup, as well as the notion of all of the unconditional love pet companions can provide. Don't rush to make your decision: only too often you hear about people who took a dog and then they realized they couldn't look after him properly.

Having a dog can be a lifetime commitment, and alongside the unconditional love and cuteness come a vast array of duties. As a pet owner, you're ultimately accountable for catering for all your pet needs like water, food, affection, and medical care should he need it. Even the best house-trained puppy may cause the occasional damage to your home, and you need to be ready to clean up after your puppy when he is sick or whenever you simply take him out for a stroll.

Be ready to come home after a day's work to find your favorite shoes chewed to a pulp or maybe to find your expensive rug in shreds. If your pet is an obsessive barker, you ought to be ready to devote a good deal of time handling the matter, or you'll have a line of unhappy neighbors ringing your doorbell to complain.

Before you sign those adoption papers, take a good look at what it actually means to have a puppy. Here are some things you should think about when making that final choice:

Should I get a dog?

If you're an athletic and energetic person or someone in your family is then yes, you can consider getting a puppy. If your family consist of busy people that are always glued to the tv or computer after work or school, a puppy might not be such a fantastic idea. Dogs require regular daily walks for no less than half an hour. You'll also need to clean up after your puppy during walks. Kids and teens eager to get a puppy will promise you and cross their hearts that they will take care of the dog day and night but these promises should always be taken with a pinch of salt. What generally happens following the novelty of having a puppy is that kids quickly lose interest and you end up looking after the dog yourself.

Dogs aren't cheap to maintain and consider getting one only if you can afford it. You need to be able to feed your pet a complete and wholesome diet, and there are a number of different costs associated with having a puppy: tick and flea remedies, kennel costs in case you go on holiday, accessories and toys along with veterinary care if your pet gets sick. Even if, hopefully, your pet never becomes ill you should still take him to the vet for vaccinations and checkups, and vet bills aren't cheap.

If you are a really busy person with hardly any free time, you shouldn't get a puppy. Dogs are social creatures that require companionship and time; they do not do well if left alone for long periods of time. Dogs left to their own devices more often than not can develop behavioral problems like destructive chewing and aggression.

Should I get a dog for the children?

In case you've got an infant or a toddler at home, you ought to postpone having a puppy. Looking after young children and infants is tiring enough without adding a puppy to the mix. They might also be incapable of interacting with a puppy correctly, which could lead to problems. Not all dogs are great with kids, and likewise not all kids know how to act around dogs.

If your child is sensible and reliable and is about 12 years old, then getting a puppy could be a fantastic idea. Dogs are wonderful for kids and they can both learn from each other . Adolescents, in particular, can benefit from owning and caring for a puppy since they are in the age when demonstrating affection to their parents could be regarded as "uncool" by their peers. Therefore, a dog could offer an emotional outlet for your kid. Teens on the other hand often go through a difficult time experiencing adolescence so they might not be consistent with caring for a puppy. If you would like to give a dog to your kids, make sure you're ready to pick up the slack if they lose interest. Children can be unpredictable sometimes, so be certain that you're ready for it.

When you've decided you can provide a puppy with a fantastic home for the rest of his life; it is time to visit your local adoption facilities to pick your new pet. Try and do as much research as possible concerning the area and the puppies out there. Speak to staff along with other puppy owners and explore some dog breeds you are interested in to detect some other characters traits or disorders they're prone to. When it comes to doing your own homework prior to bringing a puppy into your house, there are no dumb questions. Do not hesitate to ask anything that you want to know on dog ownership.

Even in the event that you decide you enjoy a specific breed's traits, then you ought to remember that each puppy is different and only because a puppy is of a specific breed famous for a given trait, this does not necessarily mean the pet will have inherited it. The Internet is filled with valuable opinions of dog owners.

Surf the net and try to get the most out of their experience.

THINGS TO CONSIDER

Before you go out and get that brand new puppy or adopt that dog, be sure and just take a couple of minutes to think of what you're getting into. There are lots of things to think about, and these 8 things can help in this procedure.

1. Dogs are social animals and so they need companionship. If you're a workaholic, then this might not be a fantastic time to get a puppy. Obviously, if you're working from home, you might be able to dedicate more time to your pet.

2. Socialize your puppy early. A puppy is considered young up to 20 months. If you don't socialize your puppy, you will likely notice that aggression or fear starts to show when the dog is between 12 - 24 weeks old.

3. Dogs have to be trained. Formal obedience training should last no less than 16 weeks. Train early, it'll be simpler for you, and it prevents the dog from creating a lot of bad habits which will cause problems later.

4. Make sure the breed of puppy that you pick agrees with your lifestyle. Do not get a terrier if you're the couch potato kind and if you'd like a puppy to go running with, do not choose a pug. Make your choice based on your lifestyle.

5. If you do not want to put up with a puppy's exhausting vitality, adopt an adult dog. It is your own choice!

6. Find a vet. Not just a good vet, however, a fantastic vet. Someone that you can trust who will provide you with the kind of service that your pet needs. Make sure you keep your pet current on all vaccines and heartworm medication.

7. Get a leash and a collar for the dog. Don't get retractable leashes. They are dreadful for a lot of reasons. Buy a leather leash that will last forever.

8. If money is an issue, you might want to look at obtaining a medical insurance program for your friend. They really can come in handy whenever there's a critical illness or crisis.

When we see folks with their beautiful puppies strolling in the park we ask ourselves "why don't I get a dog so that I could be happy just like them"? Taking care of a dog requires time, money and energy : you need to feed him, train him, provide vaccinations, and also have regular health check-ups for your doggie.

Before getting a puppy as a pet, you had better learn about dog breeds and their characteristics. That means that you may choose which breeds are acceptable for you. You will find small, medium, and large dog breeds, quiet and lively, with long hairs and short hairs, and several other characteristics. Don't forget to check with relatives and ask every single member about any pet allergies.

There are many things to consider before taking in a puppy. The dimensions of the pup are among these. If you're living in an apartment, a big dog isn't a reasonable choice because a big puppy will inevitably grow into a huge dog. Usually large breeds are also full of energy. If you don't have a garden then consider that you have to walk him at least three times a day.

If you have elderly people living in your house then you have to be extra careful. The elderly are weak and frail and a dog could easily make them fall. On the other hand, a little toy dog could be the ideal choice as they are easy to sit on your lap and stroke.

Exercise is definitely the most important thing for your puppy to get. Nearly every dog breed requires exercise, but the amount of exercise required varies . If you don't give your dog enough exercise he will have a lot of energy left in him and may end up unleashing it on your furniture. Dogs need training to become well-behaved and obedient. Without proper training, dogs will become exactly like the stray dogs we often see in back alleys. Time and patience are necessary for this particular training.

Barking is also an issue that the owner should be aware of. Dogs normally bark when are bored or have not spent their energy daily, that is why dogs love to bark a lot through the night. That's why you need to take some time to take your doggy to get exercise, play and walk. If a dog barks too much the neighbors will complain and you don't want to be in their bad books. A dog training collar may be the answer to the issue of barking. You could use the bark collar to instruct him to restrain his bark and barking only when needed.

Dogs' coats differ with every breed, and you will find short-haired, long-haired and medium-haired puppies. Dogs' hairs, exactly like a human's, fall and often get on your furniture, sofa, bed and carpeting. For this reason, you have to brush and wash the dog frequently to keep your home clean. If you do not have enough time for brushing the dog frequently, it is advisable for you to choose short-haired pet breeds. But keep in mind that your puppy will probably get cold especially in winter, so turn up the heat to make them feel warm.

Dogs love digging, peeing in flowerbeds, chewing on branches and eating vegetables in your backyard so you will want to teach them not to do that. A dog collar can help you.

You have to feed him properly. Dog food is a crucial thing to think about before getting a dog. You have to look for the ideal dog food based upon your puppy breed. As we all know, raw dog food would be the best choice for a puppy, as in the wild they would consume uncooked food. The best person to get advice from is your vet.

Legislation on dogs requires you to take care of their health. You must be ready for these expenses. Occasionally dogs can get ill, injured or inherit genetic disorders. Certain breeds are prone to hereditary genetic disorders such as: hip dysplasia, urinary bladder stones, heart disease and much more. So, make sure that the vet you choose knows that breed very well and is experienced in treating it. Should you buy a puppy from a breeder, he will be able to guide you on the choice of the right vet and give you helpful tips.

SHOULD I GET A DOG?

Getting a puppy is a choice which shouldn't be taken lightly. It's a long-term commitment where you'll be responsible for a life. Thus, before you rush to your local shelter to pick a puppy, or send a deposit to a breeder to get a new pup, ask yourself these four questions:

1. Are you sure you are financially able to provide for him, not only now but for many years to come?

To know if it is the right time to have a new pup or dog, it is sensible to have a look at your earnings, fiscal obligations, and your spending habits. Owning a puppy means not only paying the breeder for the puppy but also to provide for the dog in the future.

For at least a decade, also oftentimes even longer, you will have to cover pet food, maintenance products (bowls, leashes, collars or harnesses, grooming items, toys, etc..) and veterinary bills. Some pet owners try to save money by skipping annual vet check-ups. This is a huge mistake as getting early treatment for diseases not only increases the possibility of recovery but it also saves on costs.

Before getting a dog you should probably set up an emergency fund which you can use later on if the dog needs urgent vet care.

2. Is your house pet-friendly? Not all dogs need big yards to play and run, and in reality, toy breed puppies may be just fine in small flats. But, there are different things to examine.

You need a readily accessible outdoor place for your dog's toilet requirements. Since daily workout is very important to puppies, there ought to be a place for daily walks.

Even though puppies may enjoy a busy and big family, many don't do well with hectic or stressful families. Therefore this ought to be regarded too.

You will also need enough space, so the house (both pets and humans) doesn't feel overcrowded. Your pup or dog must also have his own place to relax, sleep and eat.

3. Have you got time to get a puppy? It is normal for owners to be away from home for school, work, or other duties. But you need to assess if you have sufficient time to spend with your new pet. Will you find time every day for walks? Grooming? One-on-one time for playing and training? Dogs love human interaction and also don't do well if isolated for long periods.

4. Does your wish to get a dog go beyond simply believing that puppies are adorable? Dogs are really adorable. However, they are also able to have snoring problems, housebreaking problems, and pee problems. A teething puppy can chew on virtually anything, and also an adopted adult might not enjoy kids.

To know if it is the ideal time to get a new dog or puppy, consider how you're feeling about taking care of a puppy every single day, as some days may be good and some may be bad.

CHAPTER TWO:
HOW TO SOCIALIZE YOUR PUPPY

Socializing your pet is an enjoyable and necessary procedure. You have to proceed with care, but since these very first introductions might impact your pet's social behavior for quite a while to come. A puppy who's granted free reign in a brand new introduction could be tough to control, whereas a person who's bullied by a different dog or fearful by tail drawing kids might become anxious in future conditions.

Step one to interacting your puppy would be to carry him on routine walks at which you may have leash controller, but he will make some buddies. A stroll around your area can assist your pet to satisfy your neighbors, their own kids, and their puppies. Getting your pet on a leash to all these introductions can allow you to keep him while he investigates. If at any moment you feel the problem is terrifying to your pet or when your pet gets overexcited, head house to get a pup break.

The following launch place for the pup Is the regional park. Avoid letting odd kids pet your pet till their parents are all right together. You can't whether a young child has allergies or perhaps if this kid may pull your pet's tail. You also ought to understand your little man might attempt to bite and play with kids because he did with his littermates. Because of this, you might have to set a muzzle on him in case you're at all concerned about this action.

Many parks possess a dog park inside them. All these dog parks are occasionally divided into smaller and larger breed places. This retains smaller strains from getting hurt by playing the bigger dogs. Even though your pet is little, whether or not she is made of a bigger breed, then you need to socialize from the major pet area. After all, your pet will probably be playing these more lively dogs if he or she's full grown.

When the dog park area is combined for large and smallish dogs or different, make sure you keep a watch out for your puppy in any way times. You'll need to wash up after him, and you'll also have to ensure that he doesn't consume anything that may lead to harm. You might even wish to walk the puppy place over to make certain that there are not any lurking hazards.

If you've got family with kids, you need to establish a specific time for all those kids to come along and fulfill your pet. Make sure their parents are found and be certain that you always remain with your pet around kids. In addition, don't allow the kids feed your pup since this may make him beg and eventually become a nuisance for you and also to the kids when they see.

Playdates are a terrific idea for new pets in addition to brand new pet parents. Meet frequently with a couple of friends with puppies. These playdates are a wonderful way to create some one-of-a-kind dog friendships. This may also offer you a chance to go over puppy particulars like vets, toys, foods an and coaching procedures.

Every pup, along with their pet, can benefit from a fantastic dog training course. Training courses are an excellent location to meet other new pet parents and their new pups. These courses will also allow you to use your puppy on some fundamental commands, including sit, down, and stay. Teaching your pup these orders at a public surroundings can help foster them listening to you with additional commotions occurring. It is going to also permit the dogs from the course to follow the case of one.

IMPORTANCE OF EARLY SOCIALIZATION OF YOUR PUPPY

Proper and early socialization of pup is essential and will save the owner a lot trouble. An under-socialized puppy within an animal shelter is much more inclined to be placed to sleep compared to the usual one. Dogs which aren't properly socialized are more very likely to come up with aggression issues. Such puppies behave fearfully to unknown items and therefore are aggressive towards strangers.

Unless socialization is completed early, the pup could develop issues which may not be simple to fix later on. Puppies don't fulfill kids, older people and other puppies will be competitive to them when mature. At an early phase, puppies ought to be subjected to as many interacting situations as you can.

Whenever you find a puppy that acts significantly towards people and other puppies or one that behaves fearfully, be aware that this sort of puppy was not socialized correctly. That's the reason why the puppy socialization should start early. Any pup that reaches age five weeks without appropriate burial is not possible to train .

The measures to follow in socializing the puppy

Since socialization should begin from a young age, the perfect time to start is when the pup is approximately three months old. At this phase in the dog's life, it's much more welcoming to new people and other dogs and can be appreciative of changing scenarios and areas in addition to distinct sounds and scents. The perfect time to select the puppy throughout the varying situations extends to approximately four weeks.

Dogs that are beyond this age may also be socialized. However, the procedure is much more strenuous and needs much participation by the proprietor. Older dogs have a tendency to be more opinionated than dogs and are less pliable.

Many dogs are still with puppy breeders throughout the period when socialization ought to be introduced. It's ideal to inquire about this before choosing a new pup home. To be successful in the efforts to socialize your pet, you need to embark upon the job the moment you bring the pup into your residence. Now the pup is ready for all those training you're able to provide, and exposing it to changing scenarios helps build its own assurance.

To achieve real success at the socialization of pup, you need to expose it to varying floor textures such as gravel, carpeting, concrete, and bud. Additionally, the pup ought to be made comfortable with various noises including vacuum cleaner cleaners and lovers. Toys accessible to the pup should arrive in varying shapes and dimensions. The pup should also meet people of varying sizes and types.

INTRODUCE YOUR PUPPY TO THE WORLD

Socializing your pet is a significant step in helping him find his own place in the realm of people and other puppies.

A puppy naturally starts socializing within the mess. But when he is taken out of the clutter, it is vital that the burial process remains in his new surroundings.

You want your pet to develop confident and comfortable in his environment. Willing to meet strangers with no cowering. Playful and lively using fresh dogs. Never competitive when encountering an unknown situation.

Adding your puppy to new people

Your puppy will live in a world filled with individuals. This is a natural element of the world. Whether it's the children next door glancing above the fence. Or the UPS deliveryman at front door. Or friends who've come to see him. You want your pet to delight in such experiences and take all of them in stride.

It's possible to assist him to socialize by exposing him to as many unique individuals as you can while he is still between 6 and 12 months old.

Invite friends or acquaintances over to fulfill your pet. Have them down to his flat and provide him a favorite dog biscuit. Be certain they don't utilize any sudden movements which may frighten him. And ensure your puppy receives compliments for taking the bite. This can help discourage bitterness and anxiety.

Take him for walks into the playground or the pet shop or on the area where he could meet new men and women. If strangers request to pet make sure, you praise your pet for his good behavior and for staying calm.

Require him to obedience classes, where he will be around other people and dogs. If your pet seems to fear in the middle of all of the action, do not force the problem. You could always try again later. But be certain that you don't guarantee him whether he is fearful, possibly. This is only going to reinforce the behavior.

Fundamentally, You would like to make the most of every chance to expose your pet to new individuals. Every new adventure will give rise to his developing confidence.

Introducing your puppy to new dogs

A puppy learns to interact with his or her siblings. This interaction helps him understand to inhibit his scratching and also create self-control. Additionally, it helps your pet to expend all of the puppy energy, which makes him less hyperactive and destructive to your home.

What do you do to assist him after he has left the mess?

Puppy kindergarten and pup training are equally excellent techniques to maintain him interacting with dogs. A neighborhood puppy training class is also a fantastic option. Or maybe you try going down to your closest dog park, that is almost always a fantastic place to work out your pup while he satisfies other dogs.

All these excursions ought to be fun, with no pressure in your pet to carry out. Allow him to socialize with all the other dogs in his own refuge.

If none of these work for you, see if you're able to locate a doggy day care service in your region. It's possible to drop off your puppy on your way to work and let him spend the afternoon interacting and playing with other dogs before you pick up him on your way house. Doing this for a week is good; more frequently, in the event that it works for you.

In the end, in the event that you presently have an older dog at the home, often, he will provide all of the drama and advise your pet requirements.

Introducing your puppy to new situations

The contemporary world is filled with stimulation for a pup. You will find auto excursions, televisions, vacuum cleaner, doorbells, screaming infants, fireworks, excursions to the veterinarian, music, and countless other brand new adventures.

Expose your pup to as a number of these scenarios as you can. The longer, the better.

As before, but don't push him to those adventures. Allow him to deal with them in his or her leisure. When he responds with dread, do not give him the wrong message from reassuring him. This just reinforces his anxiety and will help it become even more challenging for him to cope with additional new scenarios.

Socializing your pet should be an enjoyable procedure. Keep after it, and you'll have a serene, positive, and friendly family partner.

CHAPTER THREE:
UNDERSTANDING DOG PSYCHOLOGY

Most people will have undergone some type of dog psychology. Dogs have a means of getting us people to do precisely what they desire. The unintelligent puppy you understand are going to have the ability to beg for food from you with that look in their eyes, which you just cannot resist.

Having lived together across generations, puppies have learned to speak with people and let's them know what they desire. In case your dog thinks it is time for a stroll at the park, then he will bring his leash. If he wishes to play fetch, then he will bring you his ball . All activities we all take for granted nevertheless reveal the puppy is capable of learning complicated behavior.

Even though dogs may comprehend a surprising number of body and verbal language, pet psychology, and also how they process information is rather different from us people.

They have a greater ability to see in reduced light and can pinpoint correctly both smells, and sounds, and they interpret cause and effect in a very different manner.

Associating a stimulus with an answer is quite a bit more persistent in puppies, but people have the capability to alter an undesirable reaction.

Suppose you pick up his leash; he will think he is going for a stroll then also pick up his ball, and he will likely know he is going for a stroll and to play catch. But in the event that you then pick up his food bowl, he will be totally confused and not know exactly what to do , mind you would I?

Should you follow a specific pattern of events frequently, your puppy will learn what is coming , but he cannot know whether that series of events is busted. People can adapt to those changes, and puppies do not process the data in precisely the exact same manner.

Dogs can find commands by adhering to the tone of the voice and translating hand gestures which accompany these controls. Sit, stay, come, lie down, are clear examples, but puppies may also be educated to more intricate behavior as rescue dogs for the blind and support dogs reveal.

Though it's possible to educate dogs all types of things, occasionally what appears obvious to people, like not eating a dead bunny, you might not ever have the ability to instruct your pet. They cannot relate the reason for eating the bunny, being the consequence of this upset stomach that occurs later.

Just recall dog psychology and how what they believe is different from the way we know life, and even we attempt to view our dog occasionally as individual, to them, we're just another dog.

Dogs aren't human beings should not be treated exactly the same as people. By recognizing that puppies will need to be treated otherwise, you're on the very first step to educating your pet and comprehension puppy psychology. Among the most fundamental things that people have is understanding. Dogs don't read papers, paint images, and if they really do watch telly there, understanding of TV differs. Seeing things isn't the first priority to get a puppy; hence they have another means of getting around in a regular environment.

How puppy 'see' using their noses

It really is a fact that a puppy 'sees' using its nose along with a misconception a dogs nose is much bigger than a people since it seems younger. But in the event that you truly examine the face of a puppy's nose, it's actually much smaller. A puppy's nose has more tissues than the usual people, thus making it more powerful, many experts estimate up to 50 times more powerful. Therefore, it might be quite true to state that a puppy 'sees' using its own nose. They say that a few dogs may also smell salt. All living beings have a specific smell that's peculiar to this individual, and puppies are especially great at picking and additionally leaving their distinct smell or odor.

How puppy 'see' using their ears.

With regards to your dog's hearing, they're miles ahead also. We've got all noticed the Galton whistle but never heard it. This whistle was a vital victory in police crime-fighting components in which the puppy could be predicted from the quiet whistle, just by means of the offender none the wiser. On account of the simple fact that dogs may even move the muscles inside their ears, they're able to home in on certain noises and cancel other noises. We've got been in the situation in which our puppy won't come back when called. This is not because the dog cannot hear us calling; however, they just have steered their hearing where.

How good is your dog's eyesight?

It is always been noted that dogs see in black and white; however, this isn't necessarily the situation. However, it might be the situation that colors do play a much lesser part in the lives of puppies. Among the critical features using a puppy's sight is a puppy's eyesight focus is on transferring objects instead of static objects. This may be accustomed to the benefit of their dog handler simply by using motion as a means of encouraging your pet to go back, instead of just watching your puppy with his ears not listening or pretending to listen to. By increasing your hands since you call to your dog, you're encouraging your pet to pay additional attention.

To communicate with your pet and comprehend the psychology of your puppy, you have to have each one these variables into consideration. To have a great comprehension of your dog's behavior and terminology you want to check out the body language of your puppy, the way they maintain themselves, their own entire body, ears, eyes as well as their facial expression. You can view anger, joy, sadness, And fear on your own pets facial expressions and how that they hold their tails and even down to the way their coat is standing in their own backs. By bringing all this together, it creates perception you cherished pet a bit simpler.

STAGES OF DOG BEHAVIOUR TRAINING

Many individuals have difficulty with their pet being disobedient. Dogs can be quite tricky to take care of an occasions, and may as far as we adore our four-legged bites buddies, sometime we only need to shout and lock them out of sight.

Training applications are available on the market from group college to professional dog trainers who can come to your residence and spend time with your pet working on the issues you have with this.

There are 3 phases your dog may be in regard to its training.

The 3 thirds of dog behavior training are:

Blank canvas

Pound pup

Teaching an old dog new tricks

Blank canvas - the simplest time to educate your dog. As a pup a couple of days older, we can start to mold and shape our pup together with all the behavioral traits we need it to possess. Using techniques which are tried and examined for finest outcomes.

Pound puppy - Once we get a dog in a couple of months to two years of age. If you receive a puppy that's state 1-year-old, with no formal instruction, it's a broader procedure to program him, and teach him proper behavior.

Teaching an old dog new tricks - You know how the saying goes. Nonetheless, it's possible. It requires some perseverance and an extremely organized strategy. But in the conclusion of the process, there's really a sense of achievement. Particularly in the event that you rescue a puppy in the pound and figure out how to incorporate it in your loved ones.

How can you determine which point you dog is now at?

Clearly, the blank canvas is a clear one and simple to recognize. If your pet is merely a couple of days old, directly from the pet shop or by the breeder, then you've got a fantastic benefit.

Yells, you shouldn't hesitate to execute your puppies training and execute all of the methods you can from 1.

Establish out rules that are clear, before you get your pet home, and adhere with them. If you do not your pup will probably get confused later down the trail when you attempt to begin educating them doggy manners.

By way of instance, leaping up on the couch . If a puppy is permitted to do so as a puppy, then once he starts becoming a bit larger and doing harm to the couch, you request him to cease. Your pet won't know it is wrong to get it done, and you'll begin to have difficulties.

Recall: Dogs are pack creatures, and they feel much more comfortable and secure with a transparent authority and rigorous set of principles. Rules put by you, the pack leader. They'll respect you, and you'll get along superbly without needing to scold them.

The lines are slightly fuzzy when we speak about:

Pound pup vs. teaching an older dog new tricks.

Occasionally it is dependent upon the breed of your pet, your puppy's character, and the area of any training that the puppy has had in the past if any at all.

In the event you do the fantastic thing of rescuing a dog or puppy in the pound, attempt to get as many details in the pound as you can.

This may be difficult since the majority of the time; stray dogs really are only abandoned without motive. But the team in the pound will have the ability to inform you a bit about the puppy you've selected. This will set you on front when you buy your pet home.

After home, things will have to move really slowly. It might feel as you're getting nowhere, but the more the puppy is together, and you reveal it empathy and enjoy, the faster it will come about.

Recall: many dogs which come in the pound is going to have been mistreated, so it's a true trust problem coming home to a different owner.

It is important to set up confidence with a rescued pet gradually. It's imperative not to push yourself to the dog. The creature will start to find you out when they've learned to trust you.

Many puppies have been food pushed, so using snacks to build confidence can provide help. Consider stepping back a little after placing a deal on the ground. Avoid eye contact. It's necessary to praise them as soon as they take the cure.

Total whichever point that your puppy is at or anything kind of puppy you choose to get. Coaching is really a challenge and needs a reasonable bit of attention from the initial phases.

ODD DOG BEHAVIOURS

Does your pet do bizarre things you cannot describe? It is absolutely normal for pets to reveal odd behavior, which their owners do not know - creatures have various methods of attempting to inform their owners items. These acts could possibly be amusing occasionally, but the majority of the time that they leave you perplexed.

Here are some ordinary bizarre dog behaviors, why they occur, and what you can do to manage them:

Licking

We all understand a lick out of your pet is equal to your kiss. But for puppies, it is more than demonstrating affection. If a dog gives birth, then she licks her dogs to wash off them and also to groom them. Since the puppies grow, the mommy pops on them as an act of love. When your puppy licks you, then he's telling you that he frees you, and you're the boss!

Sniffing other dogs

This is most likely among the strangest things . Dogs sniffing each other's bottoms is equal to individuals shaking hands - it's a process of greeting. The main reason the bottom has become easily the most popular region which gets sniffed is since it's the strongest odor.

Peeing from excitement

Dogs receive the most enthused when they greet their owners in the door or whenever they meet folks. Oftentimes they pee themselves from delight - an act normally exhibited by dogs that are yet to understand to control their bladder. Everything you could do is to encircle your pet beyond the door if you come home before he's housebroken.

Circling their sleep spot before lying down

You have probably noticed that your furry friend circle his mattress or the place where he waits until he slides down and become comfy. This behavior go far back to their own ancestors that burst their sleeping areas to frighten insects and bugs away and to tap grassy patches.

Moving crazy after a toilet

All pet parents have undergone this their runs like mad after each bath. The reality is that dogs locate the sensation of wet fur uncomfortable and odd; that is the reason why they do everything they can to shake off the feeling. Everything you could do is to assist your pet dry up his fur quicker. Dry his fur just as much as possible using a towel or even better, use a hair drier, particularly if your pet has long hair.

Though dogs do things that we cannot describe, we must acknowledge that these strange behavior is really adorable and fun.

FACTORS THAT AFFECTS DOGS TRAINING

Whether you have experience of pet ownership, are a new dog owner, or are all going to become a dog proprietor training your pet is just one of the most significant aspects you want to think about. Likewise, if you presently have a puppy with behavior issues, afterward dog training is indispensable.

But, knowing you want to train your puppy and really training your puppy are two completely different matters. Exactly where do you begin?

To successfully train your pet, you have to think about and understand some vital aspects of dog behavior. Knowing and understanding the following 5 aspects will really boost your pet training.

1. The roots of puppies . Dogs are in nature descended from modern-day wolves. Even though domestication has dampened or removed several attributes, some essential all-natural instincts still stay. Like wolves, dogs are pack animals. What exactly does this mean?

Well, there are Numerous traits which derive out of becoming a Pack animal. The vital ones as soon as it comes to instruction are puppies are naturally social; they're utilized to regular, and they're utilized to some societal arrangement (i.e., the alpha person).

As interpersonal creatures Dogs thrive on the interaction with different dogs. A puppy doesn't believe you as a person but instead a funny dog. Thus, dogs thrive on the conversation with you. Exactly like a wild wolf, then rejected from the bunch, in case you starve a puppy of the interaction, then they will get unhappy and really agitated.

When it comes to instruction, you can use this to reward or punish your puppy. Interacting with your furry friend (e.g., tapping, encouraging/excited speak, etc.) may be as much reward as snacks of meals. Likewise, ignoring your puppy (e.g., turning your spine, stern talk, placing them in a different area, etc.) could be quite a harsh punishment to get a puppy. It's certainly better than beating them.

Much like all animals (including individuals), dogs thrive on regular. Should they understand what and when they're inclined to be doing particular things, then they're comfortable and relaxed. They understand what to anticipate and aren't confused by changing conditions.

Training must also adhere to a regular. Pick if the best period of the day is ideal for you to prepare your puppy and stick at the time as possible as you possibly can. Your pet will soon enter a pattern of hoping to be educated in say 3pm daily and will be ready for if coaching period comes. If your puppy is prepared and hoping to be educated, then it goes without mentioning that they'll really train much better.

Within a bunch, There's obviously the alpha male. The puppy, which leads the bunch, protects the bunch and finally ensures that the package is emptied and fed. As previously mentioned, a dog sees you like a funny looking dog rather than a person. For a fantastic pet owner, you definitely have to be the alpha male. How many character programs have you ever noticed in which the alpha male has been contested by one of another could be alpha male? Similarly, your puppy will probably likely be difficult you to be the alpha man - that really is really a natural urge for them.

You Have to establish yourself Since the alpha man from the start. Supplying interaction, food, punishing bad behavior, outspoken, and body speech all go towards maintaining yourself as an alpha male. If your puppy doesn't believe you as the alpha male, then they won't listen or act in your training directions.

2. A puppy's memory. Most of us know that critics have brief memories. But you might be amazed to understand that puppies also have brief retention memories. If you were able to inform something, it's very likely that from the following day or even a couple of hours after, they are going to have forgotten. However, needed (or paw) dogs have unbelievably good memory. This essentially means that when your puppy is able to associate something with everything, you let it then it will probably recall what you told for a long time to come.

By way of example in the event that you told your puppy (presuming you could talk doggy speech) the chocolate snacks have been in the cabinet your puppy would likely forget this inside a couple of hours. But in the event that you revealed your puppy in which the chocolate snacks were, then repeating the phrases 'chocolate snacks', each single time you stated chocolate snacks,' it'd likely go right to the cabinet. It might also look for the cabinet every couple of hours for the remainder of its life searching for the chocolate snacks, but that is not the purpose.

Therefore, If training your puppy, you will need to associate with the instruction issue with something. For instance: if you're teaching your puppy to sit down. If you connect the term 'sit' by putting your puppy to sit back and then providing them a benefit. Repeat this a couple days, and soon, your puppy will connect your control's it' using it sitting and getting a reward. The challenging bit is disassociating the benefit - inquire why virtually every puppy will obviously sit whenever you have food on your own hand?

3. Doggy terminology . Despite remarks over, We can't talk doggy dogs and language can't talk our language. This can be important if it comes to training. You need to select words for orders that you and your puppy will recall. Be cautious to not select very common phrases or your puppy will be readily confused if this term keeps emerging inside the center of a paragraph. A frequent term frequently utilized in dogs would be 'encounter.' For this particular instance, it could be better to work with a keyword model or blend come here' to one word.

The Main Thing is that when you choose a word to get a command to stay with it and remain constant; otherwise, your pet will end up confused.

I know it can be difficult, particularly when you come home to a TV pulled off the cupboard, to constantly utilize keywords when speaking to a puppy. Your puppy doesn't talk human language and will just understand what these few words you've trained it with will be (along with the tone you've used). Therefore, in case you get started using different words or distinct tones, your puppy won't understand.

For case in point: imagine someone talking for you personally in a foreign language requisite directions to the town hall. You cannot understand a word they're saying they get increasingly frustrated, speaking in a quicker and faster language. Is it the fault you cannot know them? Are they becoming angrier when you've got no clue what they're saying? What's the problem? Exactly what can I perform? In the same way, when you have not trained your pet to know exactly what 'sit' is and you also get started shouting'sit,"down back legs,' 'down,' and can it be that your pet's fault it's considering you perplexed and increasingly fearful.

4. Puppy behavior . The same as babies, dogs don't understand the way the world works or how they're supposed to act inside that world. They have to be educated and learn what's good, bad, wrong, or right.

A healthy and happy pup Will be a package of power, desperate to research as far as they can as fast as possible. Dogs don't have great eyes which could see hands or things which may truly feel the intricacies of things. Rather they have noses which may smell mouths and things which may chew things.

While this may come through instruction and overall aging, and the significance of this is that you need to be patient and know where your puppy is coming out of and why it does what it will.

5. Construction and pleasure . While I've in a roundabout how touched these two over, no pet training advice could be complete without mentioning both of these facets by themselves.

But you opt to train your puppy, as with regular, you need to have a structure to your practice. In case you've not trained a dog before, just how can you know if a puppy can begin learning how to sit, stay, etc. and if it could run to the local store and select the paper around for you personally?

You have to know what it's you really wish to train your puppy to finally be in a position to perform and what measures you want to choose to reach there. Personnel dog trainers, dog training classes, and dog training manuals can do that. As for me, I would rather train my dogs and think that ultimately you build a lot stronger bond with your pet. Additionally, your puppy is more obedient for you as opposed to the coach. But in the least, and especially in the event that you haven't ever trained a dog before, I would advise buying a dog training manual.

The small quantity of money to get a puppy training manual, when compared with this time you'd waste looking for totally free internet tips which are going to be a combination match of instruction and won't offer the construction, is simply not worthwhile. Over this, time saved in practice and the final result of a trained pet for the remainder of its lifetime (approximately 15 years) is worth a lot greater than the price of the most elementary training manual.

If you personally and more significantly. Your puppy don't like training, then you won't ever properly prepare your dog. Coaching will take more and be much tougher. When you begin training your puppy recall, they're likely to become a pup, and also at that era, they all wish to do is to run and explore their new world. Be adaptable with the period you intend to devote training. Attempt to maintain training brief, but when your dog is apparently very enjoying it, then become well prepared to prepare for more. Likewise, if your puppy will simply not concentrate, then Possibly abandon it for a little before heading back into it. Having a regular and structure for your practice, your puppy will soon discover that if it comes to instruction, they should concentrate for a brief amount of time and certainly will be better able to achieve that.

FOOD FOR BETTER DOG BEHAVIOUR

Altering a dogs behavior is a procedure that can take months or years, then you will find sometimes you simply can not do anything else besides handle the behavior that your dog is revealing. Regrettably, there are no magic wands to enhancing undesirable bad behavior . Each time I'm asked to visit a customer's home, I must attempt and work on the matters which can give them the fastest improvements in their own dogs behavior.

Many of us would expect me to begin here with a strict training plan; all these are significant but not as far as that which I think is most likely the fastest and simplest approach to better your dog's behavior. Where I begin is any illness / injuries, when both of them are OK, then I proceed quickly onto nourishment. Nutrition for a puppy is your single most significant thing you may utilize to boost your dog's behavior.

So how do nourishment enhance your dog's behavior, and why's it important? Firstly, let's begin with the comprehensive food marketplace or what I refer to as the food supplement marketplace. Since the beginning of foods that are complete, the planet for puppies has begun going downhill; we finally see more assumed modern-day dog associated disorders than in the past. These food businesses are making millions from you daily by utilizing fancy advertising for you to think their message during the next business.

Dogs have been omnivorous carnivores and consequently are assumed to eat a more balanced and varied diet, substantially the same as we're. Too much of a single food is great for us; we all will need to have equilibrium to keep us healthy and fit. Imagine if we had been to just drink those meal replacement beverages bodybuilders and other athletes beverage daily, weekly. For the remainder of your lifetime, what could happen? I will pretty much guarantee a drop in health. Among the things which would have the drop-in health could be mood swings, sluggishness, possibly spurts of energy, as opposed to a continuous level playing field of vitality. These are a few of the items you'd like to locate a fantastic quality complete meals or meal replacement, suppose that it turned out to be a bad excellent nutritional supplement?

Utilizing such things as barley and wheat or bulking out it with sugary goods, also let's not forget that the all-important E levels and additives, how could this influence behavior? To be able to alter a dogs behavior, we have to have the ability to observe the true puppy; the true dog means that it should be about the meals it had been born to consume rather than the bad excellent ones guy has made for them to consume.

As I have said, functioning in the behavior trade, I want to locate the fastest way to assist the customer. I am now able to state that through carefully observing several scenarios, I constantly observe an improvement in behavior after put on a pure diet. A number of the unwanted effects of the pure diet is that the dogs bathroom begins to resemble exactly what it must look like and smell like, little firm and hard stools which are relatively odorless.

Other people incorporate a general brightness of their dogs fur, decreased dandruff, and a pure repellant of all flees to list a couple.

However else does this kind of diet assist your puppy

Let us take a peek at puppy aggression. Dog aggression is just one of the most frequent behaviors I have asked to assist together, and why? Because this is part of the world.

Through analyzing the physiology and anatomy of the puppy and during listening to additional experts, I have begun to understand that dogs that have anxiety develop in ligaments and migraines, show further aggression. The main reason for them demonstrating that is like you with a permanent hassle; you will be grouchy since it hurts.

By allowing our puppies to chew sore bones and attract massive lumps of raw beef aside, they're in reality working the muscles together with anxiety at the end result in this is that they get to discharge this undesirable pain.

Today you could say why not I simply give my pet a cooked bone in the pet store? Nicely you can do so, but firstly it's splinters, second, there's not any pulling activity to operate people neck muscles, and thirdly it is not raw, such as nature planned.

WHAT TO DO WITH DOG AGGRESSION

There is a great deal of info out there about puppy aggression and several experts in tackling these issues in puppies, but perhaps you haven't read it or learn about these so that I will attempt to also provide you a few tips which might assist you when you're facing this huge issue with your pet.

Aggression in dogs is much more common than we'd need it to become and can be thought to be the most essential problem to be managed by pet owners should they own a puppy which shows signs of the behavior. As a matter of reality, dog aggression was regarded as the chief reason dog owners attempt to seek out assistance from experts due to the fact that they don't appear to have the ability to repair the issue themselves. Special knowledge and training must perform it successfully, and many individuals who have dogs do not take some opportunity to understand or aren't conscious of the significance of the knowledge, therefore that they always finish relying on the specialists.

I guess. It's essential we know what the expression aggression actually means, since there's also a great deal of misinformation concerning this and lots of dog behaviors are deemed competitive if fact they might not be.

We could encircle the meaning of aggression In various behaviors of different origins, which happen in a variety of conditions. That sounds obscure, right? We'll explain it a bit more, especially with illustrations, however.

If we put ourselves for a minute from the uncontrolled and watch animals in their natural habitat, so we'll recognize instantly that nearly all wild creatures will reveal signs of aggressive behavior should they believe their lands or offspring have been endangered, for example, obviously, their own physical health.

Female wild creatures will also kill whenever they believe their infants are at risk.

When we transfer ourselves into the "civilized" universe we Live at, and I wonder how people keep calling ourselves civilized in over 1 facet, we'll also see the exact same sort of competitive behavior is employed to be able to shield, point out limitations and set hierarchies. Countries even utilize the dangers of aggressive interventions so as to attempt and restrain others from any sort of undesirable moves.

When we come to consider dog aggression, then It's important to see it is not a word which has one significance; this is, the competitive behavior won't necessarily be exactly the exact same. We might observe a selection of behaviors and will observe that puppies will typically frighten first, and when feeling threatened at all, will wind up attacking the origin of the fear. If by chance that they wind up in a wrong situation, that competitive behavior may only end suddenly.

When we enter the domain of puppies showing competitive behavior towards people, it's crucial to note there are lots of distinct manifestations of this aggression instead of necessarily all together, such as jagged teeth, growling, barking, compelling the individual using its nose, snarling, snapping, nipping, charging in the individual free of contact, and ultimately, different kinds of snacks. You can find more indications; however, I feel these will be the most usual.

Moving back to this question of what related to dog aggression, for example, just the puppy because equation is lacking half. Not merely are the conditions to be considered, but quite importantly, the puppy owner herself or him.

Dogs aren't competitive simply because. There are always causes of this behavior and sometimes, physical causes of this, like if there's damage to specific areas of the mind or ailments that create a good deal of pain.

The very first thing one ought to search for would be the motives. Are there something in the case the dog has been included that may have triggered the competitive behavior? Can it be another creature or person that it may have responded to? How, where, and when did it occur? Was there a specific action occurring the creature may have responded to? Can it be suffering from any sort of illness in the moment? These, along with other details, need to be taken under account so as to comprehend the reason for this behavior. That will give the proprietor a clearer thought or insight to the motives and this way, arrive at the appropriate decision from that to begin so as to fix the aggressiveness.

People always look for the fault in other people, and also in the example of pet owners, taking into consideration the issue only lies from the puppy is a large mistake. Whenever you don't have the sufficient knowledge to educate and comprehend dog psychology, then you will most likely employ the incorrect steps to fix what you might think about an aggressive behavior and won't also include yourself at the explanations for why it's behaving the way it's.

Dog owners need to understand that love is critical to give when they want their pet to feel accepted, but that's only one thing. Good training in puppyhood is the perfect foundation, and studying how to handle situations where the dog can reveal inappropriate attitudes is also crucial.

It has been stated many times that dog and human psychologies aren't similar. That's quite accurate, and we shouldn't attempt and restrain aggressive behaviors in dogs the identical way we'd use with a youngster, for instance.

I think the very first thing you must do is identify the main reason behind this aggression: can it be territorial, protective, defensive, possessive, predicated on fear, societal, redirected, dependent on frustration, gender-related, because of stress, predatory, according to responses to specific people or creatures, based on responses to objects or sounds, as well as age. The list of motives, as it's possible to view, is very long and essential to understand so as to use the proper steps.

CHAPTER FOUR:
WHAT IS A DOG BITE

This bite scale includes 6 levels beginning with degree 1, described as a puppy growling, showing teeth, staring, or even ripping. The very first amount of aggression doesn't incorporate a physical bite because aggression has been defined as any action that's supposed to intimidate, frighten or physically harm another person or dog; it becomes our starting point. A degree two bite is when the dog performs one bite (making contact) without a puncture. A degree 3 bite is one bite from 1 to four punctures, every round 1/4 inch heavy.

Oftentimes the harm a puppy causes as it gets into a squabble with an individual or another pet is decided by the puppy's obtained bite inhibition. It's thought this bite inhibition is a behavior learned when the puppy is a pup during its initial 4 weeks. When a pup interacts with its littermates, suckles too hard or bites something the reaction it receives from its own mother, dad, or siblings, allows it understand how to control its bite. Why else would your pup have sharp teeth? They aren't yet old enough to need them for chewing bones, fighting or searching for food.

So why do dogs bite?

Well, it is a basic dog communicating behavior. The bite may be for a few reasons. To begin with, if they're angry, fearful, or worried, they can't just write to their regional commissioner expressing their displeasure. Second, that is what puppies do. When they play with the bite, causing no harm. Thirdly, individuals aren't always kind to puppies, and puppies utilize natural biting behavior to make space between themselves and also any perceived or real threat. In case you've got a pet that has great learned bite inhibition, and it gets into a normal tussle with a different puppy, the bite won't lead to any harm.

There are four phases a puppy exhibits as a warning system. Each degree has its own threshold. Oftentimes, as soon as a dog really gets around to scratching, it's attempted all its puppy communication to indicate that something isn't right. When first signals do not function, then the puppy is made to bite, especially if their way to escape the hurt is obstructed. When a puppy freezes, this can be a very clear warning to quit doing what it is you do. Every time a dogs growls, it's escalated the seriousness of its own communication.

If attempting to communicate using a growl is ineffective, a dog can snap, and when that warning is not heeded, your dog might bite. If a dog snaps, its goal is to frighten and to not make contact. A puppy's reflexes are really much quicker than ours, which when a puppy plans to make contact, they generally will.

If we handle these signs of dog aggression, that may be emotionally stimulated, with forceful or violent measures, all we succeed in doing is increasing the degree of aggression. If a puppy is demonstrating aggressive indications since it's fearful, worried, or in pain, we can't fight it by utilizing physical aggression; all we do is worsen the issue. The fantastic thing is that lots of the indications you could be experiencing with your pet are easily remedied using specialist procedures and techniques.

The important factor to bear in mind, as a pet dog owner, is that in the event that you find any behavior from your puppy, like staring, growling, biting or snapping contact a professional dog trainer that are going to have the ability to assist you to know what your furry friend is attempting to tell you personally and help you produce a strategy to alter the unacceptable behavior. If the behavior is left untreated, it could become progressively worse. Do not wait until your puppy is biting a degree two or 3, before you call the pros. The prognosis remains great to fix your pet's behavior, but the dedication needed to alter this degree of behavior is tougher, and at a minimum, your dog becomes a social responsibility.

WHY DO DOGS BITE?

Unlike what you may think, size often does not matter in regards to injury brought on by dogs. It doesn't matter at all if a dog is large or small, male or female, old or young. A dog of any size could bite, whether it's an octogenarian or even a very young pup. Dog bites can occur any time. The cutest and cuddliest pup or even the very best and most adorable family pet could bite if provoked.

Dogs bite for many reasons, but often it's as a response to something happening around them. It normally requires an external stimulus. When a puppy feels a situation as stressful or threatening, it might bite to defend its territory. It doesn't necessarily need to be a vicious dog to cause terrible dog bite accidents. When your dog is fearful or startled suddenly, they might lash out by biting. When a scenario is perceived by means of an animal to become threatening, then the response is to lash out by attacking the individual or other dog who's regarded as a hazard.

Dog bite attacks can occur because a puppy is truly fearful or has been assaulted themselves. Dog bite accidents frequently happen following a true threat to something or someone that they care for. They could bite to protect something that's beneficial for them, for example, something like their cousins, their meals, or something as straightforward as a toy. Dog accidents often happen when a relative is under assault, and also the dog is behaving aggressively to guard their hold and nearest and dearest.

Sometimes, dogs can reach out and bite because they are not feeling well. This might be attributed to something such as an accident, or the puppy might be rather ill and suffering with an illness and could just wish to "lick their wounds" and be left alone to heal.

Playtime can suddenly become an opportunity for the dog to become competitive. Dogs, especially puppies, can nip or perhaps bite through a session of play. While nipping throughout play may be enjoyable and stimulating for your puppy, it can, on occasion, be very dangerous for individuals. Steer clear of considerable wrestling or entering a match of tug-of-war with your furry friend. Rather than a fun sport, these kinds of actions can often cause your puppy too become overexcited, which may bring about a critical nip or a serious bite.

Knowing what to do with dogs can surely stop dog bite accidents. Educate yourself and your loved ones, especially children, about the way they need to behave around a dog. In preventing dog bites, being educated is essential.

DOG BITING PROBLEMS

Dog biting issues can happen to any dog!

Dog biting issues can occur to any proprietor, and a great deal of individuals neglect to even feel this may ever occur to them. While everyone feels some amount of regard for a large, snarling dog, they're becoming far too complacent with their own dogs. Have you got confidence in your pet in he would not bite anyone?

Would the words my puppy wouldn't hurt a fly come to mind? Most of us feel our dogs are so good-natured they wouldn't bite, till they prove us wrong. Dog owners will tell you that their puppies are totally safe with children. When I was young, I had been unlucky to be bitten, and it's left me feeling quite wary of any puppy I work with. When your child is bitten, it can make them fearful, a condition that can continue into their adult life. This can readily be brought on by the smallest nibble.

A puppy biting injury may lead to some significant puncture wounds to the sufferer. My episode just left me with a bruised arm. A bit of nursing and a couple of months of psychological scarring and the consequences have disappeared. However, the majority of individuals do not come off from a dog attack as luckily as I really did.

The unpleasant fact is that it can happen to anyone. Sure they don't place themselves into a scenario that could instigate a dog attack. Dogs do not attack unless provoked, right ? Not often. It is true it will take a while to acquire a generally mild-mannered puppy to bite the causes are not as evident as you'd believe.

So why is it that dogs bite?

Breeding and individual provocation aren't the ways that specialists see would be the reasons why puppies bite. Some breeds of puppies are said to bite more than others; nevertheless, dogs now have had several years as a family pet. We've been attempting to breed the ideal dog for several decades now.

Here's a limited list of a few of things that you should bear in mind to avoid getting bitten by a dog:

- Do not touch their food while they're eating.
- If confronted by a dog who seems like he'll bite, remain calm, and move off rather than towards the puppy.
- Never wake a dog up, particularly when he's making high pitched sounds like he's snoring or dreaming in his or her sleep.
- A puppy will secure his territory and attack any unknown visitors.
- Should you find two dogs fighting, do not attempt to separate or interrupt them; they might lunge at you without actually being aware of it.
- When your dog is sick, he's sometimes unsure of what's causing it and could blame you.
- Pets become fearful just like people any dog may bite if it believes it's at risk.
  Should you would like to stop your puppy from chewing something attempt to divert his attention until you can take the item away.
- Should you stare at a dog in the eyes, he'll notice this as a battle of dominance. When your dog is growling avert your eyes and back away slowly.

To stop dogs biting starts with the puppies handler. Do not leave matters to chance and adhere to these parts of information to prevent your puppy from biting.

- Have your puppy spayed or neutered when possible. Not only does this prevent many sorts of health issues in life, it radically lowers the degree of aggression levels in most dogs.
- Allow your puppy or dog to encounter as many distinct dogs, individuals, and surroundings as possible.
- Locate an expert dog training college and begin to train your puppy.
- See your veterinarian on a regular basis and maintain all of his vaccinations current. Get your pet accredited, chipped, and stay current on all of his paperwork.
- Always keep your pet on a leash if he's outside. Your pet ought to be kept on your property, and you ought to restrain his access to the road.

With these ideas, you'll have a joyful life together with your pets; also, he's not as likely to bite someone else. This is not a speedy fix, and you'll have to use this information all of the time and potentially for the remainder of your dog's life.

ELIMINATING DOG BITING PROBLEMS

A lot of dog owners encounter dog biting issues. These occur most frequently in young dogs and maybe solved quickly if a person uses a suitable training procedures. This guide will give you a few basic methods you can use to significantly decrease the quantity of biting from your own puppy. You have to see that biting is a pure element of each dog's lifestyle and can be used not just in a competitive manner, but also as a kind of drama and also a relief from most of the itching which pet's teething interval is connected with.

Your genuine job your pup's family

It is best to get a puppy to remain with his family before he is 10 weeks old since this can give him an opportunity to learn through drama along with his sisters and brothers what's deemed debilitating and what's believed enjoyable. By biting different dogs and being bitten by these, your pup should immediately learn to use his mouth in the ideal way. But it's frequently not possible to leave the puppy with the breeder so the dog biting issues can't be removed this way, and it's essential to start looking for different alternatives.

Where can I find new friends?

Attempt taking your puppy on routine walks and search for different puppies which may want to interact with yours. This will not necessarily be possible since other puppy owners may not enjoy it, but it is well worth trying. You might even purchase another pup and remove the issue entirely because this way is quite powerful (but costly and problematic as two puppies equal twice the effort placed into the attempting to curb biting).

I'm too tired to bite.

Another way to decrease the amount of biting seasoned is to devote some time on exercising your puppy and motivating him to move a good deal. You may begin preparing your dog or sign up to an obedience course as psychological efforts together with physical fatigue can make him very tired and not eager to bite .

Pretend your pet's mother

Even though you're at home, watch your dog's behavior and each time that he bites, you state ardently 'no more' or attempt mimicking a squeal. Quit playing with him, paying attention to exactly what he is doing. Your dog has to understand that biting equals ending of playtime and reduction in a playmate.

Why bot use a bit of Tabasco sauce?

You may also coat your palms with a powerful smelling material your dog does not enjoy or offer him his favorite toy each time he bites you. Try redirecting. He has to focus on a toy by simply substituting your hands with something to chew on (like a Kong toy).

A word or two about rewarding your dog

Even though dealing with excessive biting, do not forget to praise your furry friend for great behavior so as to fortify the desired outcomes. Screaming and hitting your dog won't work because it only brings aggression and confusion to the equation and will make it more challenging to educate your pet. Additionally, when you're training to prevent dog biting issues, don't play aggressively with him. Avoid wrestling, hitting, growling, etc. You do not need to reposition. What he's learned.

STOP DOG BITING

Are you aware that half of all dogs bite somebody or another puppy at least once in their lifetime? Dog biting is linked to pet aggression. Consequently, if you would like to prevent dog biting, you have to take care of the aggressive behavior of your pet as soon as you can. By doing this, you may prevent any lingering behavior from the dog, and you'll have a friendly and nice dog which will be of no threat towards others.

Dog biting is a phenomenon which could be shown towards individuals or other dogs. In any event, this isn't an acceptable behavior, which means you need to prevent dog biting. What many pet owners do not understand is that dog aggression, along with the implicated dog biting, is a pure reaction of creatures that is triggered by specific scenarios. So, your puppy is biting because this is the character of dogs. What should you do if you're worried or concerned?

Some people today are normally competitive and so are puppies. As you do not necessarily sting or be competitive, having the capability to release your emotions in various ways, dogs cannot do differently. This is the way nature designed animals and people. Everything you have to do would be to show your pet;

this type of behavior isn't suitable for you. The pet biting could be triggered by numerous factors, like anxiety, dominance, maternal responsibility, breach of territory or garding possessions like the food bowl, etc., being conscious of those factors is your first step to prevent dog biting. You are able to avert dog biting by preventing these scenarios.

The next thing which needs to be done to prevent dog biting would be to speak to a technical dog coach. Your pet will be correctly trained to not demonstrate any type of aggression. A suitable dog training class will teach the puppy how to become an obedient puppy rather than to bite.

Additionally, there are additional things you could do in order to prevent dog biting. One of them is to socialize your dog from puppyhood. Make it feel comfy among other puppies and people, and it will not wish to bite them later in its own lifetime. Additionally, make your pet feel comfortable with them and petting them. This way, your pet will probably be comfortable with tapping, so when strangers approach, they will not bite. Also, make certain you don't tease your dog. If you do, and then play all kinds of teasing games, then you may Activate your dog's aggressiveness, and it may bite you.

CHAPTER FIVE:
WHO IS IN CONTROL? THE DOG OR THE OWNER?

It is common sense to presume that individuals are in charge of their puppies. We feed our puppies, walk them on a leash, teach them sit-stay, and offer them the love and affection they crave. However, some dogs exhibit dominant behavioral traits, and insist on doing things their own way and attempt to take away power from their own masters. These are known as alpha dogs.

An alpha dog is more inclined to function as leader of his pack and hopes to be accountable. If your puppy regularly attempts to intimidate you or other puppies, is more competitive about meals, or is normally disobedient, you most likely have an alpha puppy.

Finally, well-trained dogs ought to think their proprietor is the alpha, and not them. Many people today believe that they can recover alpha standing above their puppies by being aggressive. This can place more pressure on the dog/owner connection and result in more issues.

Below are a few excellent ways for one to acquire control over your alpha.

Perform matches with your puppy that promote cooperative behavior. Fetch is an excellent example. If you throw a ball or stick for your dog to recover, the match can only last if the puppy brings the thing back to you personally. This reveals the puppy that you aren't an appropriate figure.

Don't play tug-of-war with your dog. This game promotes adversarial behavior, pitting you and your puppy against each other. And when your dog regularly wins tug-of-war, he's learning that he's more powerful than you and his teeth are strong, that will promote more disobedience and aggression.

In a lot of situations, alpha dogs show their dominance by simply eating before the rest of the dogs. If you are able to, try to feed your dog a few minutes after you start eating your meal. This can teach the puppy that you come first in the pack and promote patience and obedience.

Don't be too caring for your puppy. One common mistake people make with Alpha dogs is always petting, rewarding, and baby talking at the dog. Doing this provides the dog an extremely strong message - that he does not have to show you respect and obedience. This may direct an alpha puppy to yet more prominent, disobedient actions.

Take advantage of YYour affection and care as a training instrument. Teach your puppy to come, sit, stay, and mind and reward him with a minute of affection for every success. Treats can also be a potent incentive, but the very best approach to instruct your puppy is using yourself as a bonus instead of a cure which you are able to run from. Dogs certainly love our attention, and if you use it like a benefit, you will see certain results.

Use your dog's feeling of territory to clearly show your dominance. Maintain certain areas of the home as off limits to the puppy, and keep the puppy off certain furniture. If the puppy breaks these bounds, show him he has encroached on your territory. If you go through doorways and thresholds, walk-in front of your dog. The pack leader constantly walks ahead. By putting yourself in front of your puppy, you'll present your alpha standing.

EXCELLENT DOG TIPS OWNERS CAN BENEFIT FROM

1) Some individuals with very long-haired dogs every summer get their pet's hair cut by the groomers. The clip looks like a crew cut. But be cautious about doing so. Your pet's skin has not seen sunlight and can get burned. So be mindful about the length of time they lie in sunlight and after walking them. And yes, dogs without fur can get sunburned. A vet advised me of this.

2) On warm days do NOT park your car and leave your dog in it. Even for a brief period. Do NOT believe, well, it's okay I've

cracked open the window. It gets hot inside a vehicle quickly! Some cities give tickets to those who abandon dogs in automobiles. Before leaving your pet in the car to just run in to get milk in the winter, check to be sure exactly what your town's laws are.

3) If it's hot outside, put your hands on the ground, sidewalk, or street to find out whether it's warm to the touch (quickly touching with your fingertips isn't good enough). If it feels extremely hot, then wait to take your furry friend for a walk when it's cooler. Walking on hot pavement might burn the pads of his paws. If you're already on a stroll with your puppy, and she's leaping from paw to paw, then the ground may be getting too hot. Find grass for your puppy to walk on and then take her out earlier in the day when its cooler.

4) On a hot day should you leave your puppy at a tennis court along with dark asphalt where it can become extremely hot? Your puppy could burn the bottom of their paws walking on it. And if they don't have sufficient shade, they can get heatstroke.

5) If you travel in the car with your pet, on sunny days make sure that the alloy in the seat belt doesn't touch them. Hot metal burns. When it's actually hot out, attempt to park your vehicle in the shade, and take a thick white towel (white reflects) along. Put it on the metallic component of their seat belt so that it won't get so hot.

6) Don't take your puppy for hikes on warm summer days in the middle of the afternoon, particularly older dogs and dogs with long coats. A veterinarian informed me that each summer he sees dogs arrive with heatstroke. Their owners take their puppies up mountains, on paths without shade, when it's over ninety degrees outside.

This is normally midday at it's hottest. Would you like to walk in a fur coat in the heat? If you go out with your pet, be sure to have water . Start looking for a straight dog bowl in the regional pet shop. Lots of people take this to heart. My little niece told me her friend's parents took both dogs outside for an outing in warm weather throughout the afternoon. Both got heat stroke. One died, the other lived. Do not let this happen to your puppy!

7) Be cautious about allowing your puppy to sniff where folks park their automobiles. Cars can leak fluids and oils, and you don't want your puppy licking it. I've been advised by a veterinarian that dogs enjoy the flavor of transmission fluid (I think is green), which may be fatal to them. Seek veterinary aid immediately in the event that you believe that your pet has licked oil or transmission fluid.

Note: in my own town, I had been advised that you're NOT to call 911 for your perfonal furry friend. Keep your vet's phone number handy in your own personal phone book. Many regular vets aren't available 24 hours. So ask your vet for a recommendation, even before your puppy is ill, to get a crisis vet care center for when their office isn't open.

8) Ensure your dog has lots of fresh water. Give them fresh water daily. Recheck the water bowl on warm days to ensure your dog has water. Don't leave water in a bowl in the warm sunshine. The metal can get very hot, and It might burn them when they go to get a drink. Use a ceramic bowl. My ideas: if individuals nowadays aren't able to drink water from plastic bottles which have been in sunlight too long or in a hot car, then a puppy shouldn't drink from plastic water containers that were left in the hot sunshine.

HOW TO STOP YOUR DOG FROM JUMPING

Everybody has seen a jumping puppy before. You go into the dog's house, and instantly, a puppy is flying through the air to pounce on you or is bouncing up and down, attempting to get to you. As this is, it can result in a problem for a few. For those that are somewhat terrified of dogs, kids, or perhaps the elderly, a leaping dog might be a traumatic encounter that may end badly.

The initial step is to realize a dog feels the need to leap in any way. Next time you stop by a dog park, then take the opportunity to see how dogs socialize when they meet for the very first time. The very first thing that they have a tendency to do would be to attempt to sniff one another's face.

That is their way of greeting and sniffing the other puppy - in summary, learning precisely who that puppy is. In the majority of scenarios, an individual's face will be a lot higher up than the usual dog, and thus the puppy, not being educated or educated differently, will leap to attempt to get to your head to greet you using precisely the exact same method.

Unless you can be sure your dog will not inconvenience the eldrly, young, handicapped, or people frightened of dogs, this really is a behavior which shouldn't be tolerated.

Considering the domestication of dogs, they've been bred to become submissive to people. They'll have a tendency to stop doing things that disturbs us and execute commands or tasks that delight us. If you are home, your pet will most likely be very pleased to see you. He'll jump up and attempt to greet you at the most effective possible manner he understands. Among the most popular approaches that works for most pet owners is to just ignore your puppy when he's jumping until he puts his or her four paws on the ground. Give him compliments and attention instantly if he stays on the ground. It won't be too long until he knows the association involving leaping rather than draw attention.

You might need to train your puppy regularly if he's a persistent jumper. It'll be more effective to experience the routine a few days in a row compared to just to repeat it each single time you get home. If your dog starts to jump on you, then dismiss him, flex your arms, then look away and stay upright. If he settles back on the ground, commend and reward him instantly. If he attempts to jump up again, then repeat the process.

Once your dog knows what you need, it is possible to add a few additional controls. See if he'll sit once you enter the doorway. Attempt this by opening the door only a little, giving him the control , Then entering and praising when he does this. After he's got the hang of it, try this out with a few buddies and acquaintances. Consult your buddy to help out with all the coaching routines and check the way he responds To various men and women. If the dog jumps, the instruction will need to go on for a bit longer.

KNOWING IF YOUR DOG IS SICK

There is always a stage in a puppy's life when they become ill. When that occurs, we wish to be aware of the dog's condition so that we're able to treat them. Obviously, the simple fact that dogs don't have any means of speaking makes it almost impossible for all of us to see whether our pet is ill.

There are a few ways, however, to see whether they're sick.

First, pay attention to this puppy's immediate shift in mindset. If your pet is ill, he probably will drink and eat differently, or he won't eat at all.

Whenever these symptoms occur, you must immediately visit a vet. In a single day, dehydration may become fatal for dogs.

Dogs are inherently outgoing. Should they appear to get tired, then there could be something wrong with them. Correlate it together with their age, however. Like individuals, elderly dogs have significantly less energy just like older people older.

If the puppy constantly pants even without playing or exercising, he may be ill. Cancers, heart, and respiratory problems may be its own cause.

Watch if the puppy is vomiting or has diarrhea. A certain way to understand whether the puppy is ill is whether these signs do not end after a day. From time to time, nausea would only indicate that the puppy has absorbed food not acceptable for him.

But if it hasn't stopped the next day, the origin may differ. The nausea should not include mucus or blood. Nor should it be black and tarry.

A clear indication of a bladder or kidney disease are the consequences of urine. A nutritious puppies' urine is yellow-colored or is equally apparent. Sick dogs, ' nevertheless, is cloudy and does not have colour. From time to time, in addition, it includes just a tiny bit of blood.

Oral disease is another frequent illness of puppies. Gums are colored pink. Whenever there's a swelling of the teeth, it might be colored red.

Poor breath, however, is an indication of a metabolic disease. Though these appear as a small problem, it is still good to consult a vet. Dogs cannot talk. If they did, then they'd be telling you they don't feel well.

As pet owners, you need to always know when to see a vet if your pet gets suddenly ill.

The location, along with the vet's skill ought to be checked ahead. This will avert panicking for people that aren't experienced in managing sick dogs. It is better when the vet is near when a crises needs rapid support.

You should always know about your pet's behaviour. It might indicate a great deal of things. It could tell you if they're ill, it may also tell you if they are happy or depressed.

But don't be too quick to decide. The very same symptoms may occur in various scenarios.

You do not need to always watch your puppy, or regularly have them assessed by a vet. After a year is great, however, the more frequently, is better.

As they say, prevention is great and be sure to seek treatment as soon as your pet is sick.

DOG'S YEAST EAR INFECTION

Does your dog have a problem with its ears? If this is so, you aren't alone. Ear disorder is a frequent condition in dogs which may lead to pain, misery, or distress.

If you detect one or more of these signs in your pet, then he might have an ear problem:

- Strong odor around the ear region
- Regular head-scratching or tingling around the ears
- Head tilted to one side
- Discharge in the ears
- Redness or swelling of the ear flap or canal
- Soreness around the ears
- Behavior like irritability or depression

To nurse these ears back to perfect health, avoid recurring issues, and decrease expensive veterinarian accounts, follow the following 3 steps to fix your pet ears.

Measure 1: Describe the main cause of the issue.

There are numerous possibilities with regards to ear disorder. It might be a canine ear yeast infection. It might also be a fungal disease, parasites, or a foreign object in the ear, or is an underlying illness like allergies. That is the reason it's crucial to bring your pet to a respectable vet for a comprehensive examination.

Don't attempt to diagnose and treat the issue all on your own.

A veterinarian will inspect the ear canal with an otoscope. He will assess for redness, foreign bodies, tumors, along with other possible triggers. He might also take an ear swab to see under a microscope to check for germs, bacteria, or yeast infections.

It could be as straightforward as this to diagnose the problem. However, chronic ear problems could necessitate a broader examination. For instance, recurring ear infections frequently occur in dogs with allergies. In cases like this, not only will the vet have to care for the ear but also the pet's allergies.

If ear issues persist despite preventative and treatment healthcare, then it is very important for the vet to test for underlying ailments. Be conscious that chronic ear problems could indicate that your pet has a different health issue.

Are you frustrated with a treatment program that isn't working? If this is so, ask your veterinarian about the possibility of an underlying illness or additional evaluations.

Measure 2: Practice prescribed therapy program.

After your vet decides the origin of your pet's problem, he will prescribe a treatment program. Treatments will vary based upon identification.

Ask as many questions as required and be sure your understand the answer. Most veterinarians will get you through therapy to confirm that everything is proceeding nicely. Obviously, you need to call your veterinarian if you have some questions or detect an unexpected issue.

Throughout or near the end of treatment, it could be evident to you that your pet is getting better. However, do not omit recommended follow up visits to your vet if your puppy is improving. In a follow-up, the veterinarian may confirm that therapy is going well and no other course is needed.

To avoid the danger of unforeseen issues that might cost more to diagnose and cure in the future, take your pet to follow up visits.

Measure 3: Exercise preventative ear maintenance.

Owners can generally prevent ear conditions that result in costly vet bills by practicing preventative ear maintenance. The trick to a healthy pet is to keep their ears dry and clean. Clean and inspect your pet's ears at least once each week and more frequently if necessary, to avoid recurring issues.

While some dogs could have ear disorders, some breeds are far more susceptible including: dogs with long, pendulous ears like Basset Hounds, Cocker Spaniels, Labrador Retrievers, and Irish Setters and dogs that swim a lot; dogs with a history of ear disorder

For all these dogs, regular ear maintenance is crucial!

Pendulous ears trap dirt and also have a tendency to keep moisture because of a lack of airflow. Additionally, puppies that swim regularly frequently retain moisture in the ears. A warm, humid environment is the best location for a dog ear yeast infection to get started.

So keep these ears clean and dry and wait for signs that signal an issue. If you detect a possible ear problem, immediately take your pet to your vet for identification And therapy.

LUMPS ON YOUR DOG

Those of us who have puppies understand that from time to time, we'll feel a bulge somewhere on our pet's body, which seems to appear out of nowhere. The majority of the time, they're not anything more than a benign cyst, an accumulation of a swelling due to a slight accident.

Even though these lumps shouldn't worry you, you'd do well to get your pet checked by your veterinarian as an extra precaution. Since there are instances when you might be dealing with something known as fibrosarcoma.

What is fibrosarcoma? It's a kind of cancer which if left untreated, can spread to a pet's lungs or maybe into its lymph nodes. The results of the difficulty has the potential of inducing death.

Fibrosarcoma is known for a particular kind of cell known as a fibroblast. A fibroblast is a soft tissue sarcoma (a tender feeling bulge).

Fibrosarcomas can be anywhere on a pet's body. It's a category that's shared with a number of other cancer generating cells within the puppy, bones, cartilage, muscles, and fat. But they are typically found under the skin or beneath the tissue just under the dog's thighs, torso, and tummy or in the mouth area.

Why are these lumps distinct from the non-threatening bumps is the way that they grow. They are inclined to send finger-like projections like the way a tree sends out roots, and they're extremely invasive and aren't seen when taking a look at the lump (tumor) itself. They are inclined to go deeper into your dog's system, which makes eliminating them a challenge. The trick to success is the elimination of all of the areas of the fibrosarcoma and early detection.

If all of the "roots" are not eliminated, the odds of re-growth will happen and has the potential to spread to different areas of the pet's entire body.

Since there are no outward indicators, a lump (tumor) is really a fibrosarcoma; a vet should test a sample of the tissue.

It's very important that you, the owner, examine your dog regularly, at least once per month, to ensure there are no new lumps or bumps you had not previously noticed. Run your hands on your dog's whole body and check beneath its tongue and the back of your puppy's mouth. Your veterinarian will advise you regarding whether you need to keep tabs on the new bulge to find out whether it varies in its look or when he/she needs to test it farther. Sometimes a biopsy may be performed, or the veterinarian can suggest surgery or a different kind of therapy.

If cancer is located and the entire tumor can't be completely removed, your veterinarian can indicate a combination of surgery, radiation treatment, or chemotherapy.

Luckily these tumors when captured in early phases, can be eliminated and the puppy will probably be up and about behaving normally in a couple of days. That's the reason why a regular exam performed in your home is so significant; it's sort of like that old expression, "a stitch in time saves nine," and this situation can spare you and your puppy not just a pile of cash but also a quick and speedy recovery. Caught at the first phases, a fibrosarcoma can typically be totally removed and isn't going to return .

For young dogs a yearly physical is adequate, but for dogs, eight years and older, you need to really consider a twice yearly physical and include a full laboratory evaluation. The additional expense could save your pet's life and also overall save a lot of cash as a "ounce of prevention really is worth a pound of cure."

CARING FOR YOUR DOG IN ITS MATURE YEARS

The vast majority of dogs ought to live a happy and full lifetime with the right quantity of attention and care. Regrettably, a loved pet appears to leave us far too soon regardless of the 'ordinary' life span of the specified breed. While caring for your aging pet, you will want to alter his setting to adapt his comfort level. As puppies grow older, they get muscle pains, pain in their joints, generalized weakness, and, sadly, a rise in medical issues.

Adjust his surroundings to reduce this aging stress. Shelter him out of excess temperature variations. Elderly dogs cannot correct their body temperature as easily as could a younger pooch.

Make an effort to give your dog regular workouts. Remember that your dog's well-being matches his workout regimen. If your dog exhibits indications of hot flashes or simply fails exercise, you will want to make alterations to his regular regime.

Revisit his eating and diet plan and adjust it to his present requirements. As puppies grow older, they're more sedentary and just need a smaller quantity of calories every day. Vet recommended diets can be found so talk about diet with your own vet.

Elderly dogs can experience hearing loss and also waning vision. Figure out methods to aid with his security. He might not hear an approaching vehicle or view obstacle in his way.

Older dogs need dental hygiene. They're more likely to start having gum diseases and disorders. Complete dental cleaning ought to be carried out by your vet twice annually (that does need anesthesia). Make sure total blood work is completed at that time as well.

Senior dogs have additional grooming and bathing needs. Dry skin may be a standard part of growing older, or it might be an indicator of a concealed medical issue. Elderly dogs also need to have their claws trimmed more frequently. This is sometimes carried out by your vet.

Remember his age as compared to people. If he is 12 in dog years, then he can experience the very same pains and aches of a 70-year-old person. Continue scheduling the twice per year vet visits. Elderly dogs need extra maintenance and extra attention to handle their aging issues.

Supply everything you can for your very best buddy! With appropriate care, your pet could live - and - appreciate his golden years .

CLEANING OUT YOUR DOG'S PLASTIC CRATE

After your puppy has spent some time inside his plastic dog create, it's inevitable it will need a deep cleaning. There are a couple of techniques you can use to maintain your pet's plastic crate clean. This section with disclose the method I have discovered is the most effective.

The most important consideration to bear in mind is that the longer you allow your pet's plastic crate to go uncleaned, the harder it'll be to wash. If you let dirt, grime, and other natural substances buildup and eventually become caked on, then you can bet you're going to have a lot of trouble scrubbing them off. Consequently, if your pet regularly uses his plastic crate, then you need to regularly be cleaning it.

When you do your cleaning, obviously, you're likely to need to remove your pooch from this crate! If there are considerable amounts of urine or feces inside the crate, do your very best to eliminate the offending substance before cleaning and scrubbing the interiors of his crate. Next, in the event, the plastic crate comes apart, then it is going to make the cleanup a whole lot easier.

Use a clean cloth and a gentle, non-toxic cleaning alternative, like Nature's Miracle, to wash the interiors of the crate. Make sure you remove all of the dirt and buildup that's collected. As soon as you've eliminated all the dirt and buildup, rinse off and wipe away all of the cleaning solution.

After you have finished scrubbing clean all of the surfaces of the plastic crate, you can now reassemble it.

Set the crate back in its place, and put your puppy's supplies, like his toys and blankets, in the crate. The number of times you'll need to do this depends on how much time your dog spends in his crate. If you clean it regularly, you may be in a position to come up with a fast and effortless routine that could cut down the amount of time needed for cleanup and also make it a simpler experience.

CHAPTER SIX:
DOG FEEDING AND NUTRITION

Great nourishment is among the most essential aspects of raising a healthy dog. Here we have a peek at the different dog foods available and also the demands of your pet.

Most commercial pet foods are marketed to appeal to owners whilst fulfilling the nutrient needs of their dog. Some foods have been promoted on the basis of the protein content, a few derive from particular ingredients, and others are marketed because they do not contain specific ingredients such as gluten or are preservative free. You are going to want a food that fulfills your dog's needs and matches your budget. The most usual sorts of commercial pet foods are dry, semi-moist, and salty, or pouched. The dry foods have traditionally been the most economical and contain the lowest fat. The pouched pet foods have tended to be the most costly and generally include the most fat. There are off track premium dry dog foods along with affordably priced wet food. Semi-moist is becoming popular since they tend to be moderately priced but contain elevated levels of sugars.

There's been a tendency in recent decades to make meals for a particular life span, lifestyle as well as breed. It has improved the selection of meals available to pet owners and should, in principle, make it simpler (if your budget allows) to select the best food for the dog. Most commercial pet foods nowadays go through demanding feeding trials to demonstrate that diets meet a minimum criteria.

Feeding a puppy

Pups should be permitted to nurse from their mother for no less than six months prior to being fully weaned by the mother. Supplemental feeding can start as early as three months old.

By four weeks old, dogs can be fed solid food. This is a significant expansion stage. Nutritional deficiencies or deficiencies in this period of life may be more catastrophic than at any other time. This really isn't the time to overfeed or supply performance rations. Overweight young puppies may create skeletal defects like osteochondrosis and hip dysplasia.

Pups needs to be fed expansion diets until they are 12 weeks old. Pups need to get fed rations in 2-3 meals each day until they are 12 weeks old. As soon as they become adults, they should be fed 1-2 meals every day (preferably two).

Adult diets

The objective to feeding most adult dogs is a lot of care. They've already completed their growth, and also do not have the digestive difficulties of senior dogs. Generally, dogs may thrive on maintenance rations containing predominantly animal or plant-based components, provided that the portion has especially been formulated to meet care needs.

Most dogs deal nicely with a cereal-based diet though soy or even gluten are only two of those ingredients to think about avoiding if your pet shows signs of food poisoning. When buying pet foods, keep in mind that lots of pet foods from budget manufacturers are made to meet the minimum demands of a restricted dog, not the requirements of a busy dog.

Most dogs may benefit when fed foods that contain easily digested components which provide nutrients above the minimum requirements. Commonly these meals will soon be intermediate in cost, involving the most expensive manufacturers and also the most affordable pet foods that are generic. Do not pick a puppy food based on cost alone, or advertisements or about complete protein content.

Foods for elderly dogs

Dogs are considered older when they're about seven years old, and their nutrient needs change as they become older. Like individuals, a dog's metabolism slows as they grow old, and this has to be accounted for from the diet plan. As dogs age, nearly all of their organs don't work as when they were younger.

A responsible approach to geriatric nourishment would be to realize that even degenerative changes are a normal part of aging. Your intention is to minimize the possible harm done by simply taking this into consideration while your pet remains healthy.

Aged dogs will need to be treated separately. While some gain from nourishment can be found in senior diets, others may do better with the highly digestible dog food or super diets. These meals provide an outstanding mix of digestibility and amino acid material, but sadly, many are high in phosphorus or salt. Elderly dogs are also more prone to getting arthritis; it's essential not to overfeed them since obesity places additional pressure on the joints.

RAW DOG FOOD DIET NUTRITION

We certainly love our puppies! If you do not have any children, then puppies may be an incredible replacement, and if you have a family, then you know the advantages that your pet may bring!

It makes sense to want your favorite furry friend to be well cared for, be healthy and lively with a bright and shiny coat, not to mention you would like them to be an essential member of the household for as long as possible! If it comes to fixing those variables, placing your pet on a raw pet food diet is among the greatest choices you may make in ensuring that he or she receives the very best nutrition possible.

Fundamentally, a raw pet food diet is more food at its own natural condition that also offers the right nutrients, which are all important to your dog's good health. Once given in the appropriate portions, a raw pet food diet offers optimal nourishment, ensuring that your dog is healthy for a longer time. It's an excellent diet for many dogs such as young dogs, mature dogs, pregnant dogs, and dogs with ailments – essentially, any dog to maintain decent health!

What constitutes the ideal raw pet food diet which has enough of the right nutrients? To begin with, obviously lots of uncooked meats and large succulent raw meaty bones! Dogs get loads of protein in the uncooked meats that are important for a pooch's immune system and general wellbeing. As a result of eating meaty bones, your puppy receives heaps of magnesium and calcium. Both of these important vitamins helps maintain your dog's bones healthy and strong in addition to helping elderly dogs and help build powerful puppies.

It is not all meat, however. Like every balanced diet, it should also contain lots of raw fruit and vegetables. Vegetables will provide your pet with essential vitamins B, C, in addition to K, that can help maintain vision in good shape in addition to other sensory organs. A raw pet food diet also receives a great deal of fiber from vegetables that likewise help with your dog's digestive tract.

Fiber is vital to your dog's health as it helps flush toxins out in their body quickly and economically via regular bowel movements. High levels of fiber also do the preparation for their digestive tract, keeping it in the optimal condition for the next meal.

Nonetheless, there are just two more foods which you should really incorporate in your pet's diet - liver and fruit!

Liver is packed with minerals, vitamins, and other nutritional supplements like B12, iron, zinc, and omega 3 fatty acids, which contribute to help your pet stay strong in addition to maintaining its own body lean and in the appropriate weight.

Fruit, on the other hand, provides your pet with great levels of vitamin C, which aids the immune system to work at the optimal level. Free radicals have been known for causing cancer and progressing the symptoms of aging. The great news for the pet is that by consuming fruit such as berries, they get lots of anti-oxidant and these may slow and prevent disease.

The properly prepared raw pet food diet gives your pet all the vitamins and minerals it requires for each and every period of life. What's more, when prepared in the ideal proportions, you will not need to worry about giving your pet supplements or some other health additives - besides love naturally!

How can you know whether you're doing what's right? What are the ideal mixes? The ideal volumes? How do you tell if a puppy is flourishing on a raw pet food diet or suffering ill impacts?

Even though it may sound simple and all you've got to do in concept is simply give your pet raw food to consume, it isn't quite as straightforward as that! Portion control is essential, and there are tons of uncooked foods which will not create the desired result.

Putting your dog on a raw food diet may also cause some unexpected side effects, especially when you first start, so it is logical to do your homework before you get going!

THE NUTRITIONAL ROLE OF MINERALS, VITAMINS, AND CARBS IN A DOG'S DIET

Carbohydrates

The best source of carbohydrates is from cereals that a puppy eats. There are no carbs in meat. There is a tiny amount in joints and also in the liver. If our pet companion isn't getting a significant number of carbs out of its diet, its own liver is pushed into overdrive to attempt to convert sugar from its own protein reserves. When carbs are in plentiful source from her or his diet, its own body doesn't demand the conversion of carbohydrates to sugar, and its own liver isn't stressed and overworked. Moreover, these proteins may be used elsewhere. This merely suggests that the canine body, along with other functions, operate better.

Vitamins

Unlike carbohydrates, vitamins aren't the building blocks of your puppy's body. They aren't required in fueling its entire body with energy, so why are they needed? A puppy's body requires a range of vitamins for a variety of factors. Their significance is as follows:

Vitamin A is required for a lustrous coat and healthier skin. When vitamin A is missing in a pet's diet, the status of its skin is going to deteriorate, and its own coat will lack in luster. These deficiencies can also be related to a deficiency in vitamin B.

The primary duty of Vitamin B would be maintaining the immune system healthy and productive. Without it, a pet's body is more vulnerable to disease.

Vitamin C is vital in preventing hip dysplasia based on current research. This vitamin is necessary, especially for bigger breeds, which are more inclined to experience this illness.

Magnesium is a challenging mineral to consume. That is the reason why vitamin D is so essential. This vitamin supplement makes it a lot easier for magnesium to be absorbed, which leads to healthy teeth and bones.

Vitamin E functions as a powerful antioxidant. Inadequate vitamin E contributes to an excessive amount of acidity, within our pet's entire body, which contributes to different diseases like cancer.

Without the existence of Vitamin K, your pet's body is much more vulnerable to blood clots.

Minerals

Minerals are also required in the body of your puppy. There are several minerals which have particular functions to play in effectively maintaining the body's proper performance. Listed next, you will discover a variety of advantages minerals provide your pet's body:

- Phosphorus and calcium are indispensable in constructing cartilage and bones that are stronger.
- Minerals are crucial for your pet's nervous system to operate better.
- They're accountable for promoting very good muscular metabolism.
- Minerals are critical in making a healthful source of hormones.
- They're responsible for the flow of oxygen

Regardless of the significance of nutritional supplements, ingesting too much of any mineral could be toxic to your pet's wellbeing and can change the bodily features of the organs. You will find several minerals that only operate if a second is present. This is the reason why a balance should be preserved.

CHOOSING THE BEST DOG FOOD

Selecting the very best dog foods for your pet is essential to its wellness. Prior to choosing a specific food, you need to understand as much about your pet as you can to make certain you make the best and healthiest choice. Regardless of which kind of dog you've got, nourishment is every bit as crucial for everybody.

Your pet wants nutrients for to their coat, eyes, skin, and physiological functions. Nutrients are extremely crucial for mental health too. You could believe that any food will do, but this isn't necessarily the case. There are a number of producers out there who sell inferior quality dog foods, and that's certainly not what you need for your pet.

Were you aware that buying "cheap" Pet food will most likely end up costing you much more money in the long run? Whenever your puppy is not getting his nourishment, he's going to become more expensive than normal. Pets that aren't correctly fed also are predisposed toward disobedient behavior. Everybody understands the way their puppy can misbehave if he's wants attention. Possessing the capacity to differentiate between needing attention and needing nutrient-rich food is not hard. All you need to do is analyze the meals that you're currently feeding your pet.

It can help to compare while browsing for the ideal dog foods. Have a peek at what they're eating on a daily basis and then compare it to a number of the pricier brands. It may seem ridiculous, but generally, the higher a puppy food price the better it is. You'll conclude that there's a good reason behind the extra buck or two which you may need to pay. In the very long term, you are likely to save hundreds or even thousands of dollars in potential medical bills. Feeding your puppy what he needs will provide him with what it requires to be a healthy pet.

A good idea is to experiment when trying to discover the very best dog food for your pet. Look closely at how he behaves after eating particular foods. Keep a little notebook and graph his behavior for one week at one time with each food. Wanting the very best items for them as possible is simply natural.

Take note of these foods which your dog appeared the happiest with. The ideal pet food for your pet will soon render him satisfied after just consuming a small quantity. After ingestion, he will not appear bloated, will not be gassy, and will not be hungry for something else. Perhaps you will need to select a natural puppy food to spare him a lot the excess preservatives and additives.

A quality dog food will help your furry friend to build a powerful immune system, help them to keep strong bones, teeth, and joints. Odds are that they may also live longer. The very same principles that apply to humans apply to pets when it comes to health. It all comes down to picking the best foods with the most nourishment. When you venture out to select your very best dog food, do not think about cost or quantity, but rather about nourishment and quality.

RECIPES FOR NATURAL DOG FOODS AND TREATS

Most dog treats and pet foods contain compounds that have no nutritional value for your cherished pet. In addition to this, a normal box of pet food treats are priced from $3 to $4. The majority of individuals don't know that you could create your very own healthy treats and pet food in your home and also have twice as much for much less than you'd pay in a pet shop.

Here are some easy recipes for organic dog foods and snacks:

Peanut Butter Biscuits

4 cups whole wheat bread
2 cups bread
1/2 into 3/4 cup peanut butter
2 1/2 cups warm water

Mix all of the ingredients together and knead well. Roll out to roughly 1/4" thick and cut into shapes using a cookie cutter. Bake for 40 minutes in 350 degrees Farenheit oven. Allow them to cool for many hours to become hard.

Bacon Flavored Biscuits

1 10oz. Can beef consume
3 tablespoons. Bacon fat
4 cups whole wheat bread
1/3 cup warm milk
3/4 tsp baking powder
1 egg

Blend the ingredients together. Roll out to 1/4" thick and bake for 40 minutes at 375 degrees Farenheit. Let it sit and cool for many hours to harden.

Liver Treats

1 pounds. Chicken liver

1 cup graham cracker crumbs

3 tbsp honey

1/4 cup skillet

Place the components in a food processor and mix until smooth. Pour into a microwaveable container, approximately 7 to 8 inches wide. Microwave on high for approximately 8 minutes and then remove from the container. Let it cool, then cut into squares.

Homemade Dog Food

2 pounds ground beef

1 sliced beef

3 cups cooked chopped peas

1/4 cup lettuce

1 cup cooked brown rice

1/4 cup corn germ

1/4 cup brewers yeast

1 TBS minced garlic

Cook The hamburger and garlic. Then blend the ingredients in a food processor. Chop and mince until fine. Roll into little balls and let it set for a few hours. Give a few fresh meatballs every day.

CHAPTER SEVEN:
DOG TRAINING - EVERYTHING YOU NEED TO KNOW!

Many people today think that dog training is very hard. Many also feel that a few dogs are not really trainable. Both these perspectives are mistaken. The accuracy of the situation is that: all dogs are trainable, and also training a puppy does not need to be hard work. Truly, training a puppy can be enjoyable. It's obviously true that many dog breeds are easier to train than others. That which we disagree with, however, is the assertion that there are dogs that cannot be trained - since that's false. What we research then, are a few of the situations you have to do, so as to find the right method to use with your puppy.

Parameters for gauging success

You will have the practice with your puppy when you figure out how to pass onto the critical abilities to your dog within a fair timeframe.

You will likewise be recognized to have gotten the training of your puppy right in the event that you are able to ensure the dog abilities last. To put it differently, you will not be considered as being very effective in educating your puppy in the event the pooch doesn'ts exert the skills taught on a daily basis.

Therefore, the parameters ensuring achievement in pet training could comprise:

The amount of time expended to impart the vital skills to your puppy.

The abilities gained by the puppy.

Just how long the abilities are kept by the puppy.

Obviously, if you're taking too much time to pass on particular abilities to the dog, if you're making it impossible to question particular abilities in the puppy, or in the event, the puppy keeps forgetting abilities taught to her or him, it does not automatically mean that you are not doing things well. You need to keep in mind that there are just two factors at play. First is the ability, dedication, and capacity of the pet trainer. Second is the pet's natural capability - from a background where a few dog breeds appear to get' stuff quicker than others.

Historical initiation as a secret to achievement in the dogs

There are a number of skills which you may teach your dog while he or she's young. This usually means that the generally held belief that dogs under six months old should not be educated is completely wrong. In reality, there are a number of skills you'll find difficult to teach a puppy, when its older than six weeks.

It's well worth noting that unlike many humans, dogs really are (in certain ways) highly developed creatures - whose entire life skills learning procedure begins the minute they're born. That's the reason why a puppy that loses his mother at three months old could have the ability to live in the wild, whereas a baby left alone at the same age would not survive on her or his own in an identical situation.

The very best time to begin training a puppy is if he or she's learning basic life skills, so the abilities that you would like to pass to him or her will also be embraced alongside those standard canine life skills. This way, the necessary behaviors are a part of their dog's character. They'd be deeply ingrained in them. This isn't to state that an older dog cannot be trained. It's merely that you would have a more difficult time (and be much less entertaining) training the elderly pooch.

It later appears that A few of the men and women who wind up with the belief that their dogs aren't trainable are people who make an effort at educating their dogs in particular abilities too late in the puppies' lives. When the puppies don't pick up these abilities, they're tagged as boneheads - whereas it isn't actually their fault they are not able to exhibit the abilities, but instead, the trainer's fault for not having begun training sooner.

The ideal use of benefits and adjustments is the secret to success with dogs.

When we reach the nitty-gritty of pet training, it appears that different abilities and behaviors can only be transmitted in puppies through the ideal use of benefits and corrections.

The largest reward to give to your puppy is attention. And the largest correction or punishment to give to your puppy is deprivation of attention.

So, if you would like to allow your puppy to decide on a specific behavior, you want to simulate, or preferably illustrate, to him or her, then reward him or her with attention. If he acts inappropriately or if she neglects to act accordingly, you'll be penalizing him or her with less or no attention. Just taking a look at the puppy is a manner of 'rewarding' their attention. Petting, is another sort of reward. Praising the pooch liberally is still another method of giving him or her attention. True, the puppy might not understand the words; however, they are able to sense the feelings behind them. Dogs appear to get this ability.

Meanwhile, in case your dog was appreciating your care whilst doing something, and you also deprive him or her that attention the minute he or she begins doing something wrong, he or she will immediately sense the response and make the connection between his misbehavior and the lack of attention. He's likely to fix the behavior, so as to regain your attention. These items work especially well if the puppy you're attempting to train is young.

What you should not do is strike the puppy as a punishment or correction for the very simple reason that the puppy won't know that being struck is a type of punishment.

Instead, the striken pooch will presume that you're simply being abusive to her or him. If the puppy keeps doing things such as running into the street or messing up the neighbors things, you would be advisable to find means of controlling his movements, instead of hitting him.

Patience is the secret to achievement in dog training

You will not be successful in puppy training unless you're patient. You need to keep it in mind that it requires some dogs the opportunity to absorb ideas that look straightforward to us as people. There are individuals who have this misconception that you may only be successful in puppy training if you're 'tough.' To the contrary, this is one of the jobs where the 'soft approach' appears to function better than the demanding Spartan method of instruction.

Persistence is a secret to achievement in dog training

Closely associated with patience, as a secret to success in puppy training, is persistence. You will not succeed as a puppy trainer if you give up too easily for example, you try to teach your puppy a desired behavior, then give up when your dog fails to pick this up immediately.

The truth of the matter is you need to demonstrate a wanted behavior to a puppy many times, while using the needed reinforcements until the puppy finally comes to understand what's expected of it.

Consistency as a secret to achievement in dog training

This is a strategy that depends on a certain reinforcement, reward or punishment, that you have to apply regularly, so that the dog under instruction can understand what it really means. Among the worst things that you can do within the course of instruction, is to send mixed signals. After a dog becomes confused, it gets really difficult to train her or him.

GREAT DOG TRAINING TECHNIQUES

A puppy offers unconditional friendship and love to a caring owner. A well-trained pet provides more satisfaction and pleasure compared to an untrained dog. Various studies have revealed a puppy is a much happier and more satisfied creature than a one who's not.

I've been training dogs for over 25 years, and my aim is to get a pet that's happy and that I will control in almost any situation such as coming in contact with children or other creatures.

I've been effective in attaining this with zero cruelty and without even breaking a dog's temperament. When appropriate training methods are used, you'll be astonished how fast a puppy will learn how to follow your orders. Listed below are examples of several fantastic dog training methods you can use to educate your dog some basic obedience skills:

The sit command

This is the most typical and fundamental command for your puppy the learn and likely must be the very first thing that you teach him. Employing a treat as a reward for good behavior works nicely for a lot of the training. You'll require a leash attached to your pet's collar to hold him stable. Show your puppy a treat that you have on hand and hold it above his head, making him look up, then say, "Sit."

At times, by simply holding the treat above his head, your puppy will automatically sit. If he fails to sit, put your other hand on your puppy's back and lightly press down, saying, "Sit." After he sits reward him instantly with the treat and praise him by saying "Good Boy" in a happy voice. It shows your furry friend you're happy with his response to a "Sit" command. It is very important to reward him immediately once he reacts properly so that he understands why he's getting the reward.

The lie down command

After your puppy has mastered the sit command, you are able to advance into the "Lie Down" control. A treat can be used to achieve this. First, ask your dog to "Sit." Don't give him a treat for sitting. While he's in the sitting position, you ought to have a treat in your hand and place it in front of him very near the ground and say, "Lie Down." If needed, push down gently on the dogs shoulders, before your dog lies down or gently tug down on his leash. As soon as your pet lies down, then reward him instantly using a treat and say "Good Boy" in a happy voice and give him the treat to show him you're happy with his response to the "Lie Down" command. The tone of your voice is crucial to show your pet you're happy with his response to your control.

The stay command

The "Stay" command is really a little harder compared to sit and lie down. It's important to pick the proper time throughout the day to start working with your puppy on the "stay" command. Understanding your dog and recognizing if he's demonstrating a relaxed or calm character is vital. You don't want to start this training when your dog is overly excited. Much like the former training controls, it's beneficial to use a treat when teaching the "stay" command. To begin this practice, give your puppy the sit or lie down command. Once he's lying or sitting down, say "Stay" and hold up your hand like you're indicating for someone to stop. If the puppy doesn't move for four or five seconds, give him a treat and say, "Good Boy". Offer him many compliments, if he stays for the 4 or 5 seconds.

If he fails to follow your command, try again. After he gets the notion, increase the period of time he has to "Stay" until you give him the release command. You might need to replicate the "Stay" command several times and place your hand in a stop motion to get him to stay. As he starts to know the "Stay" command, gradually back away several feet, slowly increasing the distance until he masters the "Stay" command. Bear in mind, it's essential to be patient with your pet when training. If it isn't working at the moment, try again on a different day. Patience and persistence will be rewarded.

Employ traditional training approaches

When I discuss "Conventional" training methods, I'm referring to some standard methods which are important in educating your puppy.

- The Initial and most significant will be patience. You have to be patient with your puppy when teaching him new things. Much like individuals, different puppies learn at different speeds. If your puppy isn't catching on to a new command, be patient! Don't shout or frighten your puppy. At times it's far better to stop the training session and to start again the following day.

- Voice Inflection is one other very significant part of training your puppy. I refer to them as talking in a "Joyful Voice" to benefit your puppy when he reacts to a command properly. This means speaking in a marginally higher pitched tone and also in a slightly louder and excited way than you'd normally talk.

- Giving pet treats is just another common or conventional method of training your dog. Although snacks are helpful at the initial practice of a control, you do not wish to take a pocket full of snacks along with you constantly for the pet to obey your orders. You have to gradually remove the snacks after your puppy has mastered a new command and substitute it with a "Good Boy" and energetic petting.

- It's necessary for everyone in your household use the identical commands so that your dog doesn't become confused about what's being requested of him, for example, "lie " vs. "down."

- It does not matter what the command is, provided that everybody is using the exact same one.

- Eventually, they learn that your training sessions are enjoyable to your puppy. He must associate a training session together with fun. Therefore, following a practice session, you need to play with your puppy for ten or fifteen minutes, which makes the session pleasurable to both you and your dog.

Possessing a well-trained dog is just one of life's pleasures.

INTERACTIVE DOG TOYS

Interactive dog toys are available in a variety of shapes, sizes, textures, and toughness. An interactive toy is one that you can fill with pet treats, kibble, or food of some kind. When given to a puppy, it is going to keep them occupied from 15 minutes to a few hours. Such pet toys are extremely useful to your pet in various ways. These toys help to mentally exercise your pet, keeps them out of trouble, helps to clean its teeth, and keeps it busy.

Where would you get interactive dog toys?

With the expanding choice of dog toys, you will locate them just about everywhere. Pet supply stores like PetSmart or Petco is a great start. It's possible to check at a nearby pet shop, malls, at Target, Walmart, and anyplace that sells pet supplies. The best source I have discovered is online. On the internet, you will see lots of those toys to select from.

What are some great beginner interactive toys?

When you've got a puppy that has not ever been given an interactive pet toy, then I suggest starting them out with a few simpler interactive toys. Interactive dog toys vary considerably in levels of difficulty, which means you should select ones that are going to be perfect for your pet. Let's discuss a few, that will be useful, to start with.

Kong's - Located just about everywhere, Kong is among the very first companies to develop an Indoor Dog Toy. They've got an intriguing shape to them using a broad opening at one end. It's possible to start your puppy out by placing some dog food in the toy, allow your pet to watch you, then toss the Kong.

You can also set the toy down and see whether your dog begins trying to get the puppy food out. If they don't immediately, it is possible to show them that there's food there and attempt smearing a little bit of peanut butter inside. This normally gets the puppy started. As soon as they learn there is food inside, they generally look after the rest!

Tricky Treat Ball - Not really as popular as they once were and mostly found on the Internet, this is a hollow orange ball with holes on the outside of the ball. Simple to fill! Dog food readily falls out once it is moved around, crucial to keeping dogs interested to the notion of meals in small portions. In the beginning, you may need to put dog food around the ball. However, the food doesn't readily come out.

Omega Paw Tricky Ball - This ball features a great wide opening and produces a superb initial interactive toy for puppies. Dog food readily comes from the opening when moved around.

Once your pet has got the hang of obtaining food from toys, it's possible for you to begin purchasing more challenging interactive toys.

The toys will occupy your puppy for a brief period of time. If you get the kong afterward, there are many things that you can do together! Kong's, you might also fill with peanut butter or perhaps locate kong recipes on the internet. Make it harder for the furry friend by freezing the kong prior to giving it to them.

What are a few fantastic interactive dog toys to purchase?

I suggest the Kongs because there are many excellent uses for these, and they're quite durable. Aside from these, Starmark has several superb interactive dog toys, that are extremely durable. Premier Busy Buddy provides some great interactive toys too. I would not say they're as durable as the Kongs or even Starmark toys, however. Any merchandise by these last two firms are a fantastic option. It is a good idea to have three to six distinct toys around. I suggest that for a few reasons.

Your pet will not get tired of the exact same toy

It is great to split up parts of your pet's food and give your pet two or three toys at one time.

You could substitute and change toys given to a dog on various days.

What are a few great uses for dog toys?

All these toys come in so many convenient forms. You are able to give these to a pet while you're not home. Hide them in your home or lawn to keep your pet occupied in finding them. Give one to a dog while they're in their crate to keep them occupied for a while; great for when they're in a pen, or in a vehicle. Keep your pet occupied while your busy doing different things and out from beneath your feet. If your puppy is afraid of loud noises like fireworks, indulge them with a pleasant stuffed Kong to keep their attention off the loud sounds. There are lots of applications for all these toys. Use your creativity!

Strategies for filling these interactive dog toys?

A number of the toys can be tricky to fill, while some are really simple! The very best thing I have discovered is creating a home-based funnel. I use a soda or water bottle and cut off the end. Then I put the opening (from which you drink) into the opening of the toy, then add the treats in the other end!

It is easiest if you keep the "funnel" tilted a little and add the treats gradually. You can add them all at the once, cover the open end with your hands and give it a really big shake. It saves a lot of time!

DOG TREATS

Many dog owners like to spoil their dogs using a particular treat. But with the various treats to choose from, just how can you pick the ideal treat for your dog? How can you know what's safe and what is not? In the event that you choose to create your own pet treats, just how can you know what components will not be damaging to your pet? In case you provide your puppy new toys such as snacks or specific food? With so many types and kinds of treats available on the market, you can quickly become overwhelmed when attempting to choose what is ideal for your dog.

You should select a dog treat that you believe will best agree with your pet. All dogs are different, even dogs of identical breeds, and that means you ought keep your dog's nature and wellness in mind when choosing a treat and a toy. You ought to consider exactly how busy your puppy is, exactly what you intend on using the treats for your pet's wellbeing, what food allergies he could have, and just how large he is.

Many pet shops carry treats specially formulated for specific dog breeds. They're made with ingredients that are certain to be safe for the dog to eat and simple for them to digest. Though they're a bit on the costly side, these would be the safest alternative for providing your pet a safe dietary treat. You are able to essentially be one hundred percent confident that these treats can create no problem for your cherished pet.

If your puppy is actually busy or competes in shows, then he may need to consume more protein and fat in his diet compared to ordinary dogs. Extra protein and fat can give him the power he wants to be in a position to perform his or her routines. If your dog demands a great deal of energy or can be involved in any type of aggressive displays, or workout regimens, then you likely should select snacks that have added fat and protein for energy.

You should remember what is the purpose for the treats. Are they merely a wonderful method to spoil your pet? Are you really going to be using these for training purposes? Are they utilized as a tool to keep your pet satisfied when you need to be active or need to be away? If you're giving your pup a treat just to be, then make sure the treat you give him is healthy and low in fat, particularly in the event that your aim is to give it to him on a regular basis. It's extremely simple for dogs to become overweight, which may bring about an entire slew of medical issues.

Giving your pet treats for training functions can help reward him for good behavior, just make sure you make him a little treat, something he can eat in one bite. It ought to be a treat he wants and may eat quite fast, which means it's possible to continue training. Just allowing your puppy to get this distinctive pet treat as a reward for training may give it additional interest.

In case you're busy, or need to be away from home for a little while, it's a fantastic idea to leave your pet a treat that'll keep him busy throughout that time. Small chunks of food, won't meet that need, because these will all be gobbled before your car has even left the driveway. Bones and rawhide chews are often great for this objective. It may take a dog a few hours to make it through a rawhide bone. It offers him something that takes time. You're also giving him something that can help keep his dental health too. Attempt to select the one that's the proper size for the puppy. Should you select one that is too small it won't last long, and then you run a possibility of it straightening and lodging in his stomach.

If you buy a bone that is too large, he will not have the ability to grab it so he can take it elsewhere. It's necessary that you select something that won't split into smaller bits, since these could possibly be fatal choking risks to your pet, particularly if he is going to be left alone with it.

Always maintain your pet's wellbeing in mind when buying treats. Also be sure you read the labels carefully. If you are aware your pet is allergic to a specific food, find out how to read labels, and each of the alternative names it may have. Your vet will be able to help you understand what to search for to make certain that what you purchase is safe for your dog.

If you are attempting to treat your pet but are strapped for cash, you might want to try making your own pet treats at home. Many snacks can be made from ingredients that you probably already have in the cupboard, and various sites can be found on the internet that could provide you recipes and instructions. There are a number of foods that are extremely harmful for your pet, so make sure you check all your ingredients to be on the safe side.

Another advantage to making homemade dog treats, besides saving you a significant amount of money, is that you will know that each ingredient is of premium quality, so there is nothing in the treat that may possibly be detrimental for your pet.

Do not allow your puppy to eat table scraps, or let him consume any food which has onions, garlic, grapes, raisins, caffeine, chocolate, or any sort of milk products. These can cause many different ailments, ranging from stomach upset to death. If your pet has some allergies that you are aware of, make sure to not include anything that may lead to a reaction from your homemade treats.

CPSIA information can be obtained
at www.ICGtesting.com
Printed in the USA
BVHW040818240521
607637BV00012B/437

9 781914 172618